A–Z

OF

JARROW

PLACES - PEOPLE - HISTORY

Paul Perry

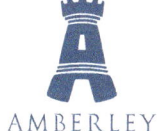

AMBERLEY

Acknowledgements

I am most grateful to the following people and organisations for the assistance and co-operation shown to me during the preparation of this book: the Connolly family, Lady Doreen Dixon, David Morton, John Joyce, Lawrence Cuthbert, Malcolm and Anthony Perry, Christine Linsley and family, John Miles, Oliver and Angela Snowden, Teresa and Tom Graham, Revd Father Gerard Martin, Andrew and Lorrain Hillas, Norman Dunn, Ray Shorting, Malcolm Miles, *Newcastle Chronicle & Journal*, Newcastle City Libraries, staff at Monkton Stadium, *Shields Gazette* and South Tyneside Council.

While every effort was made to authenticate dates etc., occasionally mistakes and omissions are inevitable and are, of course, entirely my fault.

Dedicated to my brother Malcolm for decades of endless support. His selflessness is genuinely appreciated.

First published 2018

Amberley Publishing
The Hill, Stroud, Gloucestershire, GL5 4EP
www.amberley-books.com

Copyright © Paul Perry, 2018

The right of Paul Perry to be identified as the Author of this work has been asserted in accordance with the Copyrights, Designs and Patents Act 1988.

ISBN 978 1 4456 7288 5 (print)
ISBN 978 1 4456 7289 2 (ebook)

British Library Cataloguing in Publication Data. A catalogue record for this book is available from the British Library.

Origination by Amberley Publishing. Printed in Great Britain.

Contents

Introduction	4
Allotment Society	6
Arndale House	7
Alderman Terence O'Connor	8
Belsfield School	9
Benedict Biscop	10
Bede's Well	11
Bede Industrial Estate	12
Backyard Bookmaker	13
Bent Axle and Dinky Derrick	14
Civic Regalia	15
Christ Church	16
Cornelius Whalen	16
Cenotaph	17
Charles Lennig & Co.	18
County Hotel	19
Drewett Ormonde Drewett	20
Day Trips	21
Ellen Wilkinson	22
Education	23
Football	25
Food for Thought	26
Gasworks	27
Gasworkers Social Club	28
General Dealers	29
Housewives Choice	30
Housing	31
Isolation Hospital	32
Isabella Drewett Brown	33
Industry	33
Italian Job	34

Joseph Bede Symonds	36
James Hunter Carr	37
Jarrow Instruction Centre	37
Jarrow Gibbet	38
Jarrow Crusade	39
Jarrow Metal Industries	40
Jarrow Slake	41
John Miles	42
Kino Theatre	43
Lord Don Dixon	44
Leo Connolly	45
Lambs Potato Crisps	46
London & Newcastle Tea Co.	47
Lamplighters	48
Little Ireland	49
Local Government	49
Monkton Stadium	50
Market Square	51
Modern Alternative Housing	51
Mercantile Dry Dock & Engineering Co. Ltd	52
Monkton Village	53
Masonic Hall	54
Mayfield Girls' School	55
North Eastern Hotel	56
Northern Bus Station	57
Outdoor Pursuits	58
Ode to a Crusade	59
Paper Mill	61
Public Houses	62
Palmers' Shipyard	63

Parkland	64
Pub Crawl	65
Queen Elizabeth II	67
Queen Elizabeth The Queen Mother	67
RMS *Berengaria*	69
SS *John Bowes*	71
St Paul's Church	72
Swimming Baths	72
Ship Breaking	73
Station Stairs	75
Sir John Jarvis	75
Simon Temple	76
Sir Charles Mark Palmer	77
Tyne Tunnels	79
Timber and Chemical Industries	80
Tram Service	81
Trains, Boats and Reins	82
Unemployment	84
Venerable Bede	85
Valentine Linsley	86
Viking Invasions	87
Waterfront	89
Wartime Jarrow	90
William Henry Richardson	91
Wesleyan Movement	91
Xylography	93
Youth Clubs	95
Zephaniah Harris	96

Introduction

As we get older, the passing of time seems to gather momentum. Life today moves so much faster than that of our forefathers. This realisation often leads us to stop for a moment and reminisce about how very different things were many moons ago. This book is designed to help us pause and look back at the life and history of Jarrow.

In these pages we take a look at the Gyrwy, the tribe of people who frequented these shores around the sixth century and were most likely the earliest inhabitants in the area. We trace the industries that supported and dominated the town for decades, allowing it to flourish. Agriculture, one of the town's forgotten mainstay industries, receives deserved attention, its vital contribution often being overlooked. At the beginning of the seventeenth century, Jarrow was a simple rural village comprising of the old church and monastery, a handful of tiny cottages and three farms, which covered an area of approximately 1,200 acres. Ancient maps from this time indicate three principal farms: Grange Farm was built in 1665 by Robert Ellison and covered an area from Monkton to the southern edge of the town; the second in order of date and similar in size was Curlew Farm, and appears to have been built towards the end of the eighteenth century; and the final farm referred to was Red House Farm. From these facts we can ascertain the population in 1801 of the township, which included Hedworth and Monkton, was around 1,566. These records provide evidence that a considerable proportion of the town's tiny population were largely agriculturists, farming somewhere between 1,200 and 1,500 acres.

Influential figures such as Simon Temple and Charles Mark Palmer, their influences, enterprises and contributions, also take their place in these pages. We look at the rise and fall of our town's fortunes, how it impacted the shape and personality of the town and how it affected its families and communities.

When we compare Jarrow to many other towns nationwide, it is relatively small in comparison, both in population and geographical mass. Where Jarrow differs from its counterparts is its heritage, of which so many of us are aware, and which is ancient and varied, dating back to Saxon times and beyond. Sail making, salt production and the manufacture of stained glass are just three of the lesser-known industries that nevertheless played a significant role in the heritage of the town. Lest we forget the notorious ninth-century invasions, courtesy of our Danish cousins across the North Sea, leaving behind a trail of destruction and devastation after each visit. Or the uninvited visitation of the army of William the Conqueror, who looted and burned to the ground our ancient monastery on the banks of the River Don, the former home of 600 or so Benedictine monks, and probably the most important monk and scholar of all, Bede. However, in more modern times the industrial era is equally important, thus playing its role in constructing the framework of the town's rich and colourful past.

The A to Z format has been a joy to explore, though with such a rich and diverse history to sift through narrowing down the entries for each letter has not been an easy task; for instance, whether to include Albert Road or Andison's mineral water manufacturers, or Greenbank Villas or Gallon's grocery store in Grange Road. It has been a very interesting project, differing from the usual format of local history books in several ways. Thus, my approach was different. While initially thinking to begin at 'A' and work logically through the alphabet, the daunting thought of 'X', 'Y' and 'Z' arose, so I turned heel and started at the end and was amazed to find myself with four 'Z' options to choose from.

I have spent many enjoyable hours compiling this book, losing myself among countless photographs, maps, directories and documentation, gleaning information to piece together an accurate picture of the history of Jarrow, a history that never fails to astound me. I hope this publication brings you many enjoyable hours too.

Paul Perry, 2018.

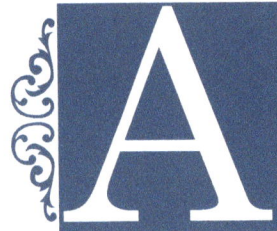

Allotment Society

Through the often difficult and challenging times of the 1930s, everyone 'pulled the rope' in the same direction, helping one another and retaining a strong sense of community spirit, enjoying themselves as best they could with pastimes such as pigeon fancying, football and dancing. The council introduced an allotment society, providing an area of land between Bede Burn Road and Springwell Road that had been sectioned off into manageable sized allotments for rent and available to any interested

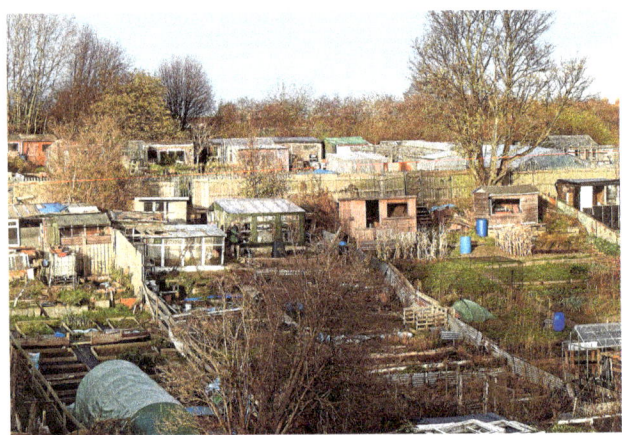

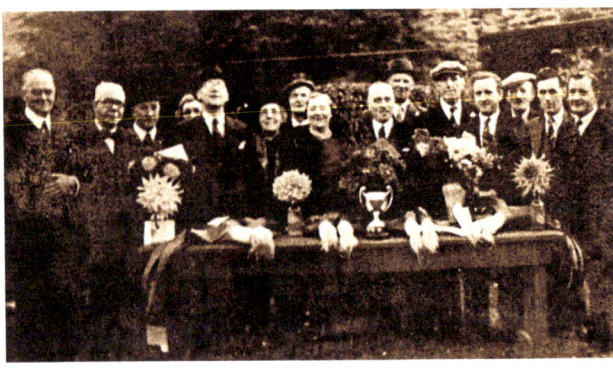

Allotment Society at Pigsty Avenue, and Monkton Leek, Floral & Vegetable Society, 1940.

parties brave enough to rise to the challenge. The eighty allotments in 'Pigsty Avenue', as it became known, were swiftly occupied. All manner of quality fruit, flowers and vegetables were produced by the enthusiastic amateurs. The Monkton Leek, Vegetable and Floral Society was founded in 1864, thought to be the first of its kind in the country and always keen to welcome new members. 'Pigsty Avenue' produced many expert growers were attracted to the Monkton Society, eager to display their produce in their annual autumn show. During the formation of the society, viewing and judging took place at the Robin Hood public house close by, owing to unsuitable facilities at Monkton. It wasn't until many years later that the Lord Nelson Inn became host to the now established show, and has remained so to the present time, with the exception of the war years when the show was organised in a nearby school (it was thought the marquee housing the exhibits would draw attention to the enemy, thus provoking an air attack). As the pastime gained popularity, the best part of the region's workingmen's clubs followed the trend by staging their own version of the annual autumn event. Alas, the CIU movement fell from popularity, as did the horticultural event, with the exception of the show at the Lord Nelson. The popularity of the autumn show is evident by the huge crowds it attracts. In 2017, the society celebrated its 154th anniversary.

Arndale House

A partnership between Arnott and Chippendale resulted in the creation of the Arndale Property Trust Co., the first company to create 1960s-style inner-city shopping centres. Arndale House, at the foot of Viking Precinct, became the centre of commerce for the centre after phase one opened in 1961. The first two floors of the four-storey building were used as offices, with the upper two floors given over for the use of an exclusive Italian-themed nightspot, Club Franchi. Continental-style nightclubs became fashionable during the 1960s and were springing up in many towns and cities nationwide attracting major stars from the world of entertainment. Nearby in South Shields, around the same time,

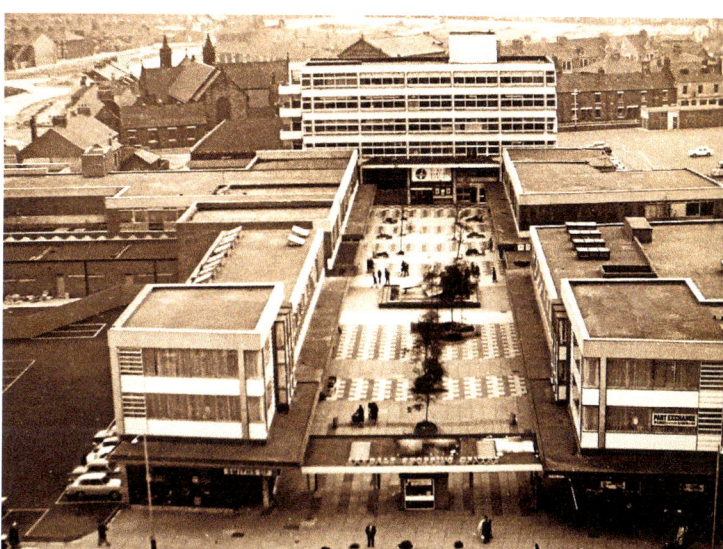

Arndale House, 1963.

the Bailey Organisation was gathering speed with a chain of such clubs, beginning with Latino at Crossgate. Back in Jarrow, and in 1961, construction was well underway of an American-style tenpin bowling centre. As the craze swept the country, Jarrow was chosen as the first venue in the north-east for such a centre. As the popularity of the pastime grew, bowling alleys were springing up in all parts of the region. In 1964, the Dogs Bowl opened in South Shields on the site of the former greyhound stadium, followed by centres in Gateshead, Newcastle and Sunderland. By the late '60s, the game had run its course and was rapidly losing popularity – the region seemed to be overrun with bowling alleys. Jarrow, the first to open, was the first to close in 1968 after a lifespan of just six years. This was closely followed by South Shields and Gateshead. A recent revival of the game saw the opening of several centres around the region.

Alderman Terence O'Connor

In a bid to help him cope with the deep sorrow he suffered at the death of his wife Rose, aged forty-six, in 1919, and of his son David, a thirty-two-year-old Catholic priest, from peritonitis ten years later in 1929, grocer Terence O'Connor, following a recommendation from the Catholic church, immersed himself in the politics and public affairs of the town. He was overwhelmingly elected to the town council and to several important welfare committees. He progressed to the enviable position of alderman and chief magistrate of the town soon after. In 1938, the staunch Irish alderman was elected mayor, and held office for the customary one-year period. During his time in office, he accepted many invitations; one in particular was from friend Sir John Jarvis to preside over a prestigious reception on board SS *Berengaria* prior to it being broken up at the former Palmers' Shipyard. The caring and compassionate grocer showed unending generosity to his loyal customers, offering them credit during the lean years of the 1930s, when Jarrow folk had little or no money and certainly no work to go to. By the summer of 1939, the popular grocer was in a state of ailing health and passed away in September the same year aged sixty-eight.

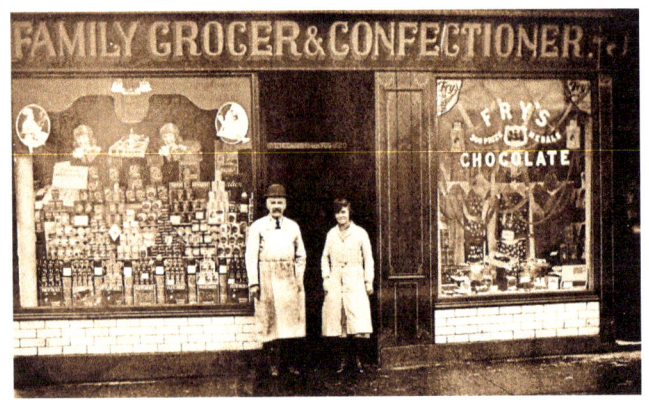

Alderman Terence O'Connor and shop assistant May Lindsay, Monkton Road, 1929.

B

Belsfield School

After the First World War, Parliament passed the Fisher Education Act under which Central Schools were authorised for the first time. This new educational opportunity was seized upon by the Parish Council of St Bede's. A sizable residence and grounds in Bede Burn Road – 'Belsfield House' – were procured for the creation of such an establishment. After the necessary alterations and refurbishment, the Central School for Girls was opened by His Worship the Mayor Robert Andison on 22 May 1920, one of the first schools of its type in the region. The new school was staffed by nuns of the Daughters of the Cross, giving families and interested parties the opportunity to take advantage of this innovative style of higher education. The school flourished in all departments and divided into four houses: Milne, Newbolt, Barrie and Yeats. Inter-school sporting activities were popular among the girls and competition was fierce, with occupants of the four houses having equal enthusiasm, especially the netball team who were presented with the silver league cup for the third successive year in 1932, at the Metupa Stadium at Monkton. Sport was always encouraged at Belsfield where cricket was very well played, but it was netball and tennis where the girls excelled during inter-house competitions. After careful monitoring by the authorising bodies revealed surprising and excellent results for the school, the sisters found staffing the school increasingly difficult, and forced their resignation. From then the school was staffed by lay teachers, with a rather large proportion of them being university graduates who received their introduction to higher education at Belsfield. In 1959, St Joseph's Grammar School at Hebburn became available, relieving pressure on many

Belsfield House.

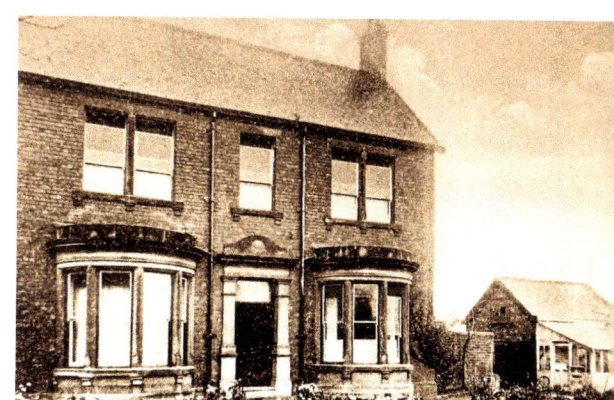

of the Jarrow schools, and the big old house Belsfield became St Bede's Secondary Modern School for Senior Boys in 1960, until it was demolished around 1974.

Benedict Biscop

So impressed with the abbey church of St Peter he built at Monkwearmouth in the seventh century, King Egfrid gave to Abbot Benedict Biscop a grant of 40 hides of land in 682 for the purpose of building a second monastery – St Paul's at Jarrow, or Donmouth as it was called then. Biscop brought workmen from France to assist him in the construction of the monastery and were the first ecclesiastical buildings in the country to be built of stone. Biscop imported glassmakers from France for the unusual practice of fitting his churches with windows and embellishing them with paintings and artefacts brought back from his many trips to Rome. Upon completion of the Jarrow Monastery, Biscop installed Ceolfrith as abbot, as he continued his perilous trips to Rome. By the year 673 Biscop was stricken with paralysis. His friend and confidante Sigfrid, abbot at Monkwearmouth, also with ailing health, was beckoned to Donmouth to ease the suffering of the dying Biscop. Sigfrid never returned to Monkwearmouth as a short time after the death of Biscop, he too was called by the Lord. The names carved on the dedication stone to St Paul's Church in AD 685 have been partially obliterated with the dirt and grime of fourteen centuries. The words themselves, engraved upon the stone above the west arch of the tower, are still legible. Much of the primitive building still survives, housing the earliest piece of stained glass known, and holds the honour of being one of this country's oldest and revered buildings. At the time of the church's dedication when it, together with the monastery, emerged from the flat marshland, the winding River Don then a crystal stream rippling past prior to its continuation to its confluence with the swelling River Tyne, must surely have been a matchless scene of tranquil serenity. The names of the abbots of Jarrow are recorded in the publication 'Lives of the Abbotts of Jarrow', which was written after the monastery

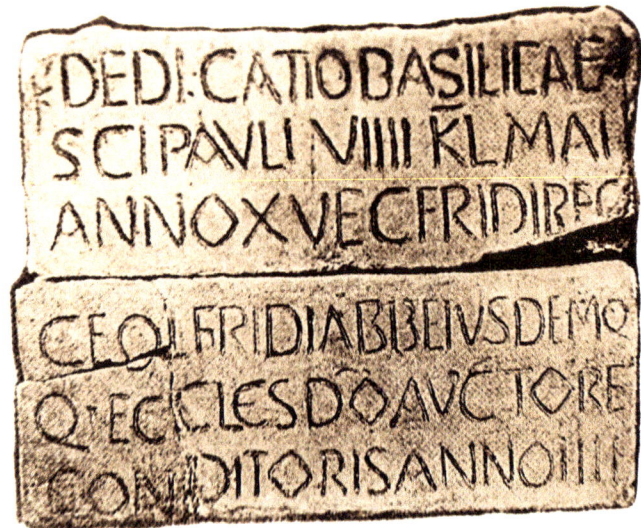

Dedication stone at St Paul's Church.

was devastated by two Viking invasions – the first in AD 794 and again in 866. During this second cruel invasion the twin monasteries at Monkwearmouth and Jarrow were looted, Jarrow so severely it was abandoned and lay derelict for close to 150 years. In AD 1075, Walcher Bishop of Durham made several unsuccessful attempts to restore the monastery without success. As the centuries passed further attempts were made to restore the decaying relics, which by this time had suffered irreparable damage. Its Roman and Saxon ruins have lain undisturbed for centuries.

Bede's Well

The ancient spring of St Bede at Monkton is more commonly known as Bede's Well. In the northern counties of England, many ancient wells and springs still exist, which from the remotest periods of English history possess a legendary and popular interest. This is identified in some cases with the Roman occupation, which merged into the early development of another civilisation, and has generally been connected with a local or titled saint. Many of these wells have been associated with peculiar customs and ceremonies from a dark and distant past. As late as 1740 it was still a prevailing custom to bring children to Monkton who were troubled with disease, when a crooked pin was dropped into the well. It is recorded as many as twenty children were brought together on a Sunday morning to experience the power of the 'magic water'. Dropping pins into these wells was more common in Cornwall, Ireland and Wales, but was by no means limited to these areas, and it is from this practice they were to become known as pin wells. For many years, it was believed that Bede's Well was a boundary marker and this could be true, when you take into consideration the location of this particular well. The Anglo-Saxon translation of Bede's Well is 'badeswelle', which loosely translated means 'the well of prayer'. In 1908, the parish council of Monkton was anxious to take steps towards the preservation of the well and to raise £200 for the sole purpose, believing the industrial and commercial encroachment of neighbouring

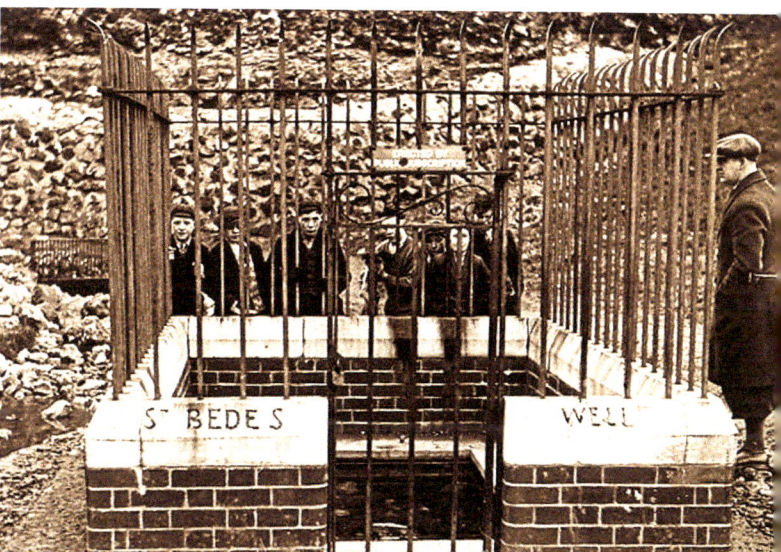

Bede's Well at Monkton.

Jarrow threatened to destroy this ancient watering place. Throughout the ages, it was believed Bede and the brethren from the Jarrow monastery used the well as its prime supply of water. As the monastery was constructed close to a water source, it is most unlikely Bede was aware of the very existence of the well.

Bede Industrial Estate

A determined Britain would never again endure the shortages and hardship that wartime brought with it. The government introduced new measures to introduce agricultural production. Farmers hurried to invest what little capital they had in new machinery, pesticides and fertilisers, and it wasn't long before the fruits of their labour and investment became evident as yields increased by a massive 50 per cent, a valuable contribution to the country's resources. By 1955, the average working man's weekly wage in Jarrow had risen to £8, with many of them having a disposable income for the very first time. Work became available for women in both shops and the factories of the

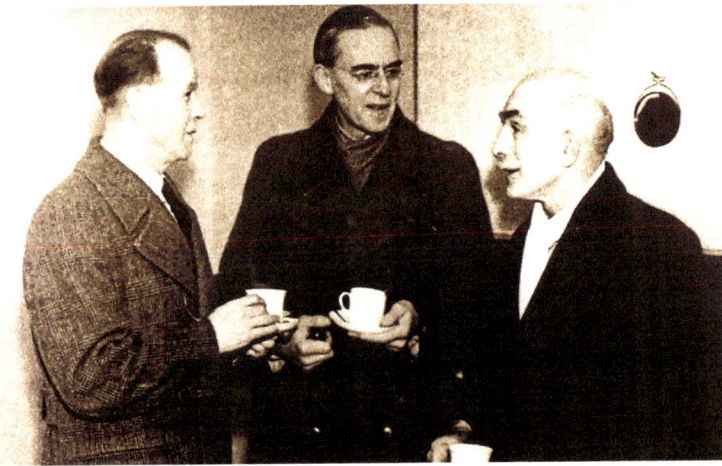

Sir Stafford Cripps (centre), president of the Board of Trade, the Mayor of Jarrow Alderman James Hanlon (left) and Mayor of South Shields Alderman Robert Longstaff visiting Bede Industrial Estate in 1946.

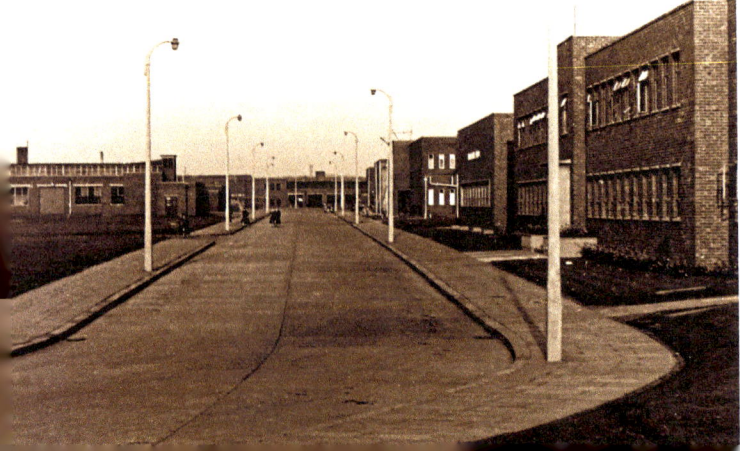

recently completed Bede Industrial Estate, with hours to suit the needs of individual families. This extra income was a welcome contribution for the Jarovians to get back to their feet. The town was once again set to ride high on the crest of an economical wave.

Backyard Bookmaker

Through the days of triumph and tragedy the most outstanding feature of Jarrow has been its people. Famous writers, singers, lords and ladies, actors, entrepreneurs, Members of Parliament, and good hard working men and women, together with an abundance of local characters and villains, have all grown up in the town, but it is the ordinary Jarovian possessing a rare mixture of honesty, decency and good humour that has given the town its unique personality. In return all are marked forever by the town and have a genuine sense of pride and affection for it. Several names and stories synonymous to Jarrow folk have evolved over the years, some tinged with sadness and tragedy and others not so, but most of which are coloured with what Jarrow lads and lasses were attributed with – humour! Prior to betting shops becoming legalised, and for a long time after, if you fancied a flutter on a horse, one had to visit the 'back yard bookie' of which there were many. The self-appointed bookmaker would sit in the wash house in the backyard and happily take your 'tanner each way'. His two accomplices, one either end of the back lane acting as lookouts, would blow a whistle in the event of a visit from the local constabulary. This so-called bookmaker was no more than a bookies runner, the middle man between the genuine turf accountant and the punter. A tip for a horse called 'Pinza' was given, which was running in the 1953 Epsom Derby, and just about every punter in the town backed it, with a large number of them betting with the popular 'Big Bud' from his wash house in the back yard of Monkton Road. His popularity rapidly declined after this particular race. The tip duly obliged, and Pinza

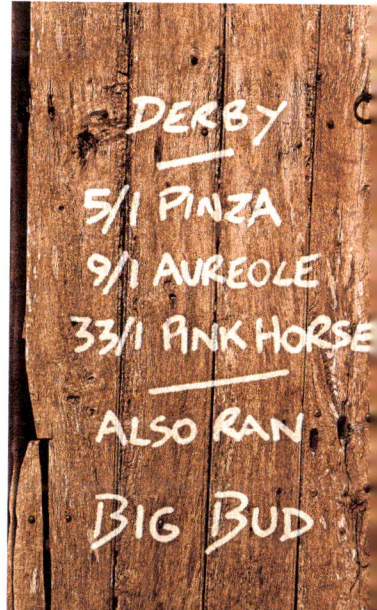

Backyard bookmaker.

romped home at 5/1 much to everyone's delight, but as punters made their way to 'Big Buds' to collect their winnings, they were surprised to find everything locked up and no one at home. As usual, the result was chalked up on the back yard door along with other runners and riders, to which someone with a sense of humour had written 'ALSO RAN, BIG BUD'. Bud had scarpered with the punters winnings. No one knows if they were ever paid or indeed what happened to Big Bud.

Bent Axle and Dinky Derrick

Many of the town's characters, although never rogues, occasionally would fall ever so slightly on the wrong side of the law. One in particular, a man with one leg shorter than the other and only ever known as 'Bent Axle', would push a squeaking wheelbarrow – with a twisted axle – from one end of Jarrow to the other from dawn until dusk, seeking out discarded scrap iron to 'weigh in' at Johnny Devlin's scrapyard at Pitt Street. He would also collect rags and woollens but pour water on them in order to increase the weight for a better price prior to presenting them to Devlin. Another of these so-called villains of the peace was a homeless and harmless but mischievous individual Martin Derrick, known to everyone as 'Dinky', who inherited the nickname from his ability to move around the dance floor with so much grace and dexterity. Forever in trouble, Dinky would find solace in the generosity of the parish priest at St Bede's Church in Chapel Road, who clothed and fed him on many occasions, and would allow him to sleep at the back of the church on cold winter nights. His luck finally ran out when the priest caught him lighting his cigarette from a candle on the high altar. From this time he lived rough, but occasionally would cause enough mayhem for the local magistrates to give him a short custodial sentence, just long enough to keep him off the streets and out of mischief. This was his assurance of a nice warm bed with three balanced meals daily over the Christmas period.

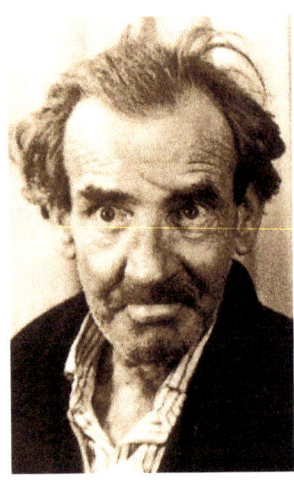

Martin 'Dinky' Derrick.

C

Civic Regalia

At the quarterly meeting of the town council in November 1875, Alderman Thomas Sheldon was elected mayor in succession to Councillor Palmer. Upon the councillor's retirement from office and duties as the town's first mayor, he presented to the council a solid gold chain of office that represents the town's close association with shipbuilding, and was to be held by the current mayor, aldermen and burgesses as part of the property of the Borough of Jarrow. An inscription on the pendant, which bears the town's coat of arms, reads 'The first Mayor of the corporate town of Jarrow, Charles Mark Palmer Esq MP gave this chain to his successors in office November 1875.' The arms of the borough symbolise the ancient association with Bede and, again, its connection to the sea and shipping. A silver and ebony civic mace bearing the arms of the borough was presented to the current Mayor Councillor Patrick Scullion in 1949, by industrialists of the town. Encased in the head of the mace is a scroll that commemorates the circumstances of the presentation.

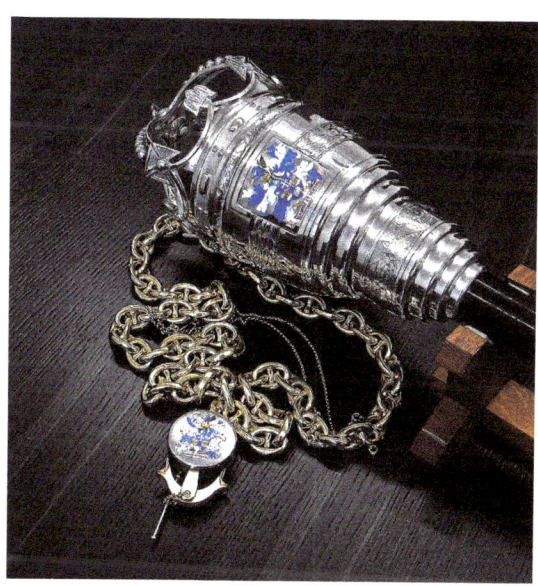

Borough of Jarrow civic regalia.

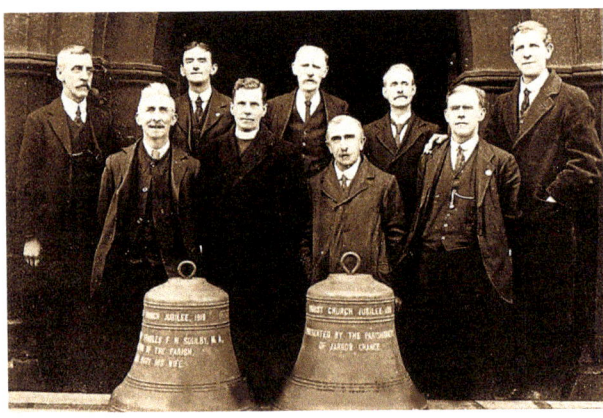

Revd Soulsby and the church council pictured at the presentation of an additional two bells on the occasion of the fiftieth anniversary of Christ Church, 1919.

Christ Church

In 1863, and prior to the creation of the parish and construction of Christ Church, services were conducted in local schoolrooms, and in 1868 Revd John Bee was appointed as the first rector of the recently formed Jarrow Grange parish. In 1869, with the financial support of Sir Walter and Lady James, the church was built, consecrated and ready for worshipers in October the same year. The tower and spire with six bells were added to the church in 1882. At the celebration of the golden jubilee of the church in 1919, Dr Moule, Bishop of Durham, dedicated two additional bells to make a full peal of eight, as a memorial to those men of the parish who fell in the First World War. No fewer than sixty rectors and curates have served the parish since its inauguration. An extract from the churchwarden's financial report of 1883 reveals an income of £165 for the previous year, with a deduction of £20 for heating and lighting.

Cornelius Whalen

Cornelius (Con) Whalen, the only son of William and Teresa, had two sisters, Ella and Rosie, and the family lived in a tiny house in Ferry Street. Con was educated at St Bede's School at east Jarrow where he made the mile-long trip twice daily on foot, and often barefoot. Records of the day reveal he was a very bright and amiable individual who was an avid reader from a young age and could often be found in his bedroom reading by the illumination of a street light. Similar to many families at that time and others of his generation, they experienced extreme hardship due to difficult family circumstances. A further blow to the young Cornelius was the death of his father in 1916, when he was aged just seven years. After leaving school at fourteen, he was expected to seek work and assist with the family finances. His first job was in the shipyards as a riveter's 'catcher' followed by a spell at the dole school where he was mentored in woodworking skills, and finally to Salisbury working for

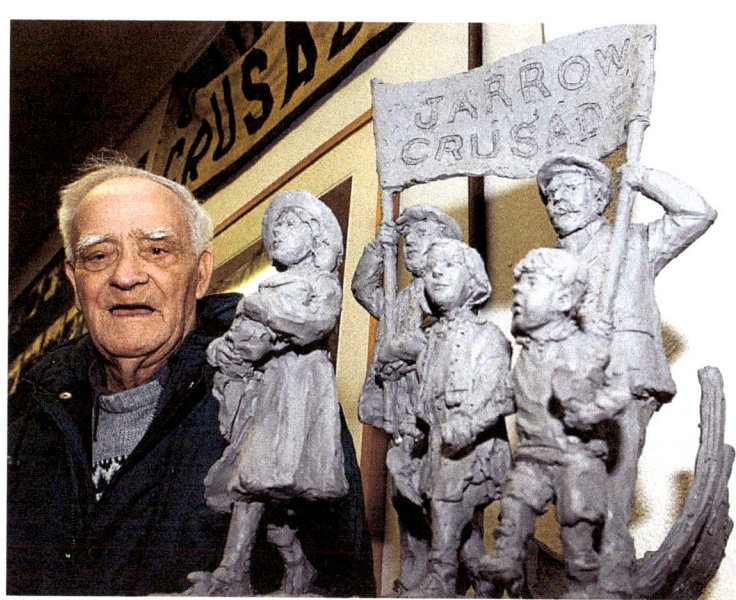

Cornelius Whalen.

the War Department. On his return to Jarrow, penniless and with few prospects, he volunteered for the 'Crusade' to London, and was selected after passing the appropriate medical procedures. At the outbreak of war, he was conscripted to Palestine in Egypt. In 1943, he married Jarrow girl Sarah Ellen Edgar with whom he had one daughter, Teresa. The very quiet and unassuming 5-foot-tall former 'crusader' was honoured with a beer named after him 'Old Cornelius' by the former Jarrow Brewery in 2002. Con passed away at the Queen Elizabeth Hospital Gateshead in 2003 aged ninety-three. The steelworks, furnaces and shipyard lights may not be burning brightly, and the 'crusade' still a bitter memory, but the memory of the last 'Jarrow Crusader' will burn bright and live forever in the hearts of his daughter Teresa, son-in-law Tom and his three beautiful granddaughters.

Cenotaph

Civic dignitaries, businessmen and members of the Masonic movement joined a crowd of 5,000 or more to march in procession through the streets of the town, terminating at Clayton Street for the solemn ceremony of unveiling and the dedication of a monument to those who fell in the First World War. Traditionally, on the eleventh day of the eleventh month on the eleventh hour a two-minute silence is observed as a mark of respect to those who gave their lives for king and country. As the years passed, the savage northern weather ravaged the 20-foot-tall sandstone monument to a degree where the inscription was illegible. Sensitive and careful restoration work was carried out in the 1990s to the sculpture, which plays an important role in the town's heritage. Mr G. Muir Ritchie, chairman of Palmers, who donated the monument to the borough,

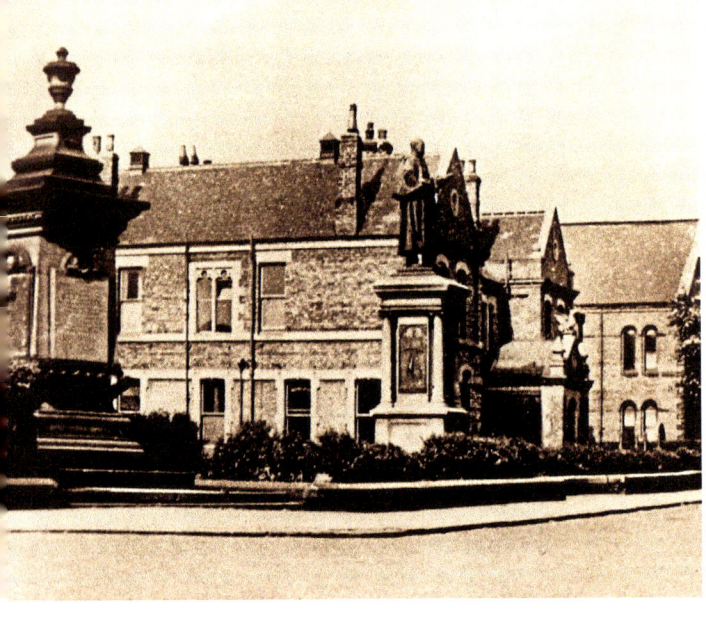

The cenotaph dating from 1921 at Clayton Street.

performed the unveiling ceremony in November 1921 flanked by a guard of honour from a regiment of the Royal Engineers. The reverend Williams, rector of Christ Church, offered prayers and following a two-minute silence, the Honourable Robert James laid a wreath of poppies at the base of the monument on behalf of the directors of Palmers. Reverend Ritson, rector of Jarrow, recited the final blessing and formalities were concluded. Upon completion, buglers from Palmers' band sounded the 'Last Post'. The mayor Councillor Robert Machin accepted possession of the deeds transferring the cenotaph to the custody of the Borough of Jarrow for safe keeping. The inscription on the monument reads 'Erected by the directors and shareholders of Palmers' Shipbuilding & Iron Company Ltd, to record their appreciation of the patriotism of 1,543 from the Jarrow & Hebburn works in joining His Majesty's forces for service in the Great War 1914–18 and in grateful and honoured memory of those who made the great sacrifice for their country, and whose names are inscribed on this monument.'

Charles Lennig & Co.

Chemical giants Rohm and Haas was founded in Esslingen Germany in 1907, producing chemicals for a wide range of industries and applications. In 1909, Haas relocated to Philadelphia, USA, to set up an American branch of the company, while Rohm remained in Germany. As the American company grew prior to Second World War, its development of Plexiglas – a type of acrylic glass – was in great demand for the manufacture of aircraft canopies. In 1955, under the banner of Lennig Chemicals Ltd, a subsidiary of Rohm and Haas developed a plant in Jarrow employing in excess of 200 personnel, manufacturing speciality raw materials for the construction and electronic industries. In 2009, in a multi-billion-pound deal approved by the European Commission, the company was purchased by Dow Chemicals. In 2014, the company announced the Jarrow plant was to be axed and relocated to China.

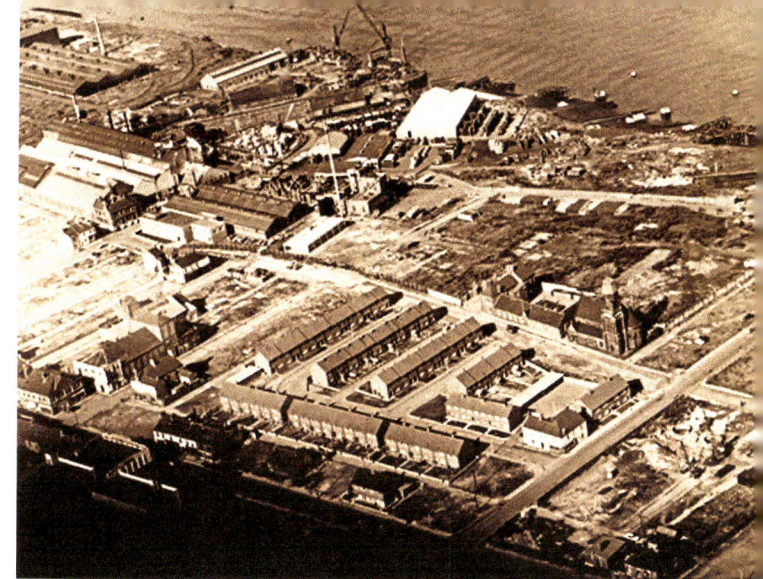

Charles Lennig Chemical works and riverside from the air, 1960s.

County Hotel

During the Victorian era, facilities for meetings by various organisations and clubs in the town were few. The usual venues for such gatherings were Lockhart's Cocoa Rooms or the County Hotel in Ormonde Street. It was the latter of these venues that accommodated the Jarrow County Rover's Club, a male-oriented association that enjoyed outdoor pursuits and fresh air. Their inaugural outing to Stamfordham took place in 1894. Another of these institutions that met at the County Hotel was the Jarrow Cycling Club. Outdoor pursuits, depending on their size, were generally held at the Metupa Sportsground at Monkton. These facilities were sponsored and given over to the town by the three major employers, the Metals, Tube Works and Palmers, and it is from these three industries that the word Metupa was derived. The venue was perfect for the inaugural Jarrow & District Floral and Horticultural Society Gala. The two-day event attracted hundreds of townsfolk and interested parties from all parts of Tyneside. Today the venue is known as Monkton Stadium.

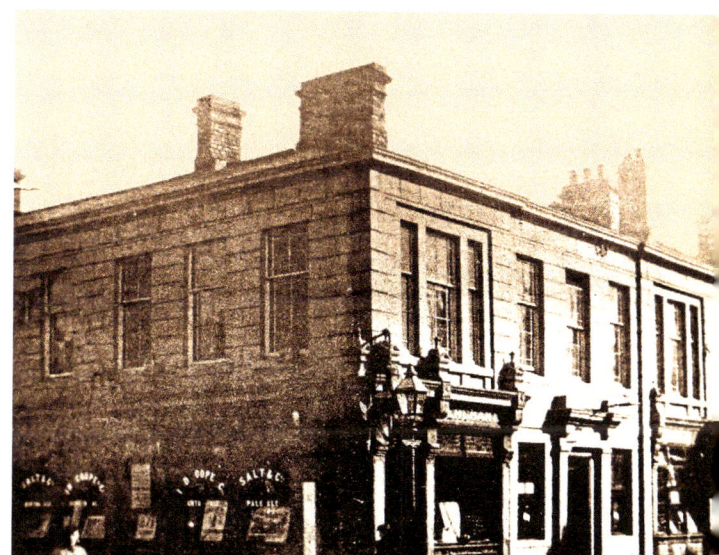

County Hotel in Ormonde Street, 1940s.

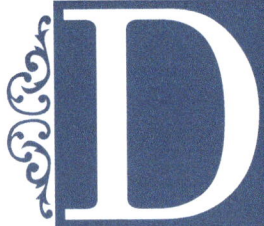

Drewett Ormonde Drewett

Drewett Ormonde Drewett was born at Jarrow Hall in 1839. In 1867, he married Catherine Mary Burrell, and later the same year he was elected as member of the local board of health for Jarrow and by 1872 became chairman of the board. The caring man was generally involved in local government through his concern for the welfare of the population of Jarrow, but was often at odds with the governing bodies with his position and as a local land and property owner. In 1895, he refused to give the town council a site for the purpose of creating parkland, though he was willing to lease the land to them for twenty-one years at a nominal rent of £1 per acre per year. The council could not agree to his proposals and decided to seek another site elsewhere. Drewett passed away in March 1910. Having no children of his own, he left his entire estate to Alfred Henry Chaytor, a New Zealander adopted by the Drewett's. In 1911, Chaytor donated a field south of Jarrow Hall to create a park in memory of his adopted uncle. The council graciously accepted the donation and in 1912 the Drewett Playing Fields were officially opened at considerable expense to the ratepayers. A park keeper, Charles Harrison, was appointed to oversee the day-to-day running of the park, and maintain the standards made by Chaytor, and soon became known as 'Charlies Park'.

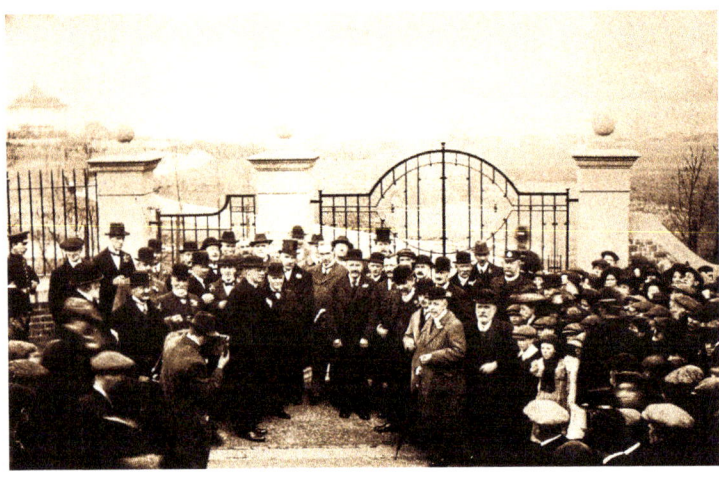

Council officers and dignitaries at the opening ceremony of Drewett Playing Fields, 1912.

Day Trips

'Back to canny auld Jarra' is a phrase commonly known to Jarrow people, a people who are now enjoying their sixty-plus years. These words were echoed as the Monkton coke works came into view, to a tune fondly remembered by anyone who chanted the little ditty, and was always followed by a verse or two of 'Oh the drivers got the wind up' as the rickety old coach with steam billowing from its radiator brought the tired day trippers home. These 'trip buses', as they became known, chugged along the granite cobblestones, often their clapped-out engines overheating and almost bursting at the sides with day trippers. These day trips played a vital role towards the welfare of the community and were nearly always organised by a couple of street residents, who would spend their spare time collecting instalments for the two bob a head day out. It was the informal simplicity of it all that made these carefree days usually to the seaside so successful. The excitement of the children was infectious as they waited patiently perched on the kerbstone for the arrival of the coach for the 9.30 departure, and at the same time desperately trying to keep their Sunday best clean. Meanwhile, mothers busy assembling a picnic of seaside sandwiches – egg and tomato – and filling thermos flasks full of sweet milky tea, for what seemed like a journey to the ends of the earth. Games, races and competitions were organised as part of the day's activities, with prizes awarded to victors of the team games. Similar to most town's in the country, Jarrow was recovering from the effects of the second war, and the cessation of an industrial boom. The precious commodity of money was scarce. But with a strong community spirit, people managed with what they had, getting by and sharing what little resources available to them.

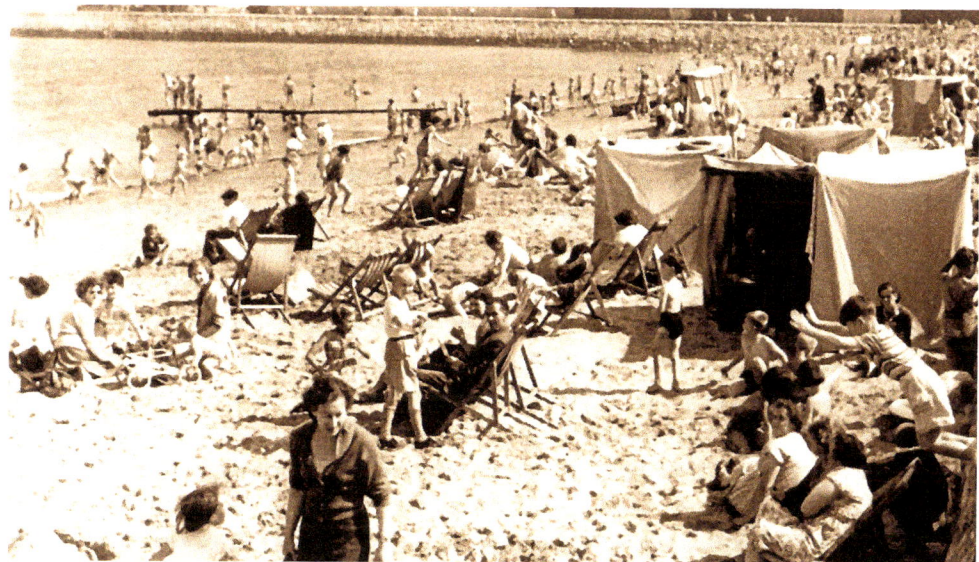

Day trippers at South Shields, 1956.

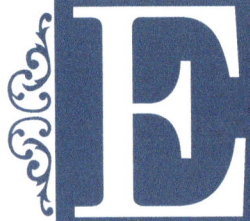

Ellen Wilkinson

Ellen Cicely Wilkinson was born in Manchester in 1891. Despite suffering ill health as a child, she was educated at Ardwick Higher Elementary Grade School, but received much of her education at home due to illness. Aged eleven, the rebellious youngster was transferred to Stretford Road Secondary School, and in 1906 began the arduous task of teacher training, where the fiery young Ellen often fought with her superiors over her teaching methods. Around this time, she realised her chosen profession was not the way she wanted to earn her living. Aged just sixteen, she joined the Independent Labour Party, and in 1910 won a place at Manchester University and was awarded a BA degree. After developing a sound understanding of politics she became a valued asset to the Labour Party movement. After a term of seven years as a Member

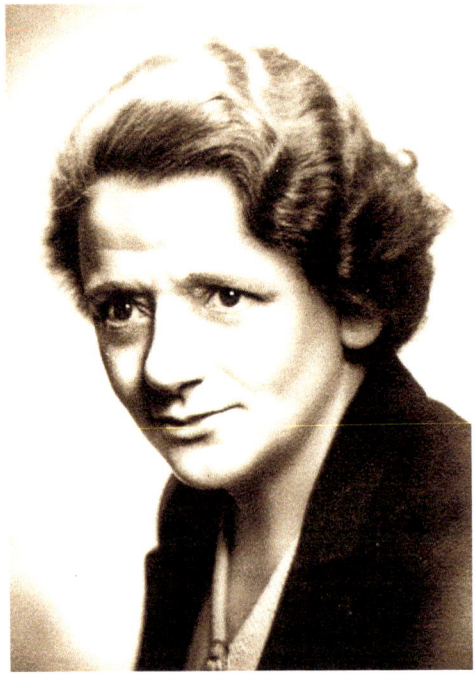

Ellen Cicely Wilkinson, former MP for Jarrow.

of Parliament for Middlesbrough East, Ellen Wilkinson moved north with a view to follow in the footsteps of retiring MP for Jarrow, Robert Wilson. She was elected as the prospective Labour candidate for Jarrow, and after a successful campaign 'Our Ellen', as she became affectionately known, became a dedicated member of the Labour movement, and the town's most memorable MP in 1935. At this time Jarrow was a town of heartbreak, a town murdered by capitalism. It was initially thought most unusual for a woman to be selected for such an important role in a male-dominated industrial area. At a Labour women's conference, she was quoted as saying 'women do not get their fair share of good constituencies'. The tiny-framed MP fought a good fight for the people of Middlesbrough and soon realised she had to fight even harder for the Jarovians, immersing herself in the town's complex problems. During the 1930s, living conditions were deplorable and death from tuberculosis was double the national average. She challenged the Minister of Health's cruel statement, 'there was no great hardship and starvation in her constituency', and verbally attacked him by quoting the case of three young men who died of malnutrition. The mighty voice of 'Red Ellen' echoed throughout Parliament as she battled for work and better conditions for her people. In a damning retort, president of the Board of Trade Walter Runciman said, 'Jarrow must work out its own salvation'. It was this crass remark that angered the furious MP and instigated the organisation of the 'Crusade to the Capital' in 1936. Ellen Wilkinson passed away after an accidental drug overdose in 1947.

Education

Prior to the introduction of formal education in Jarrow, there were five schools in the east end of the town. Meeses chemical works conducted a school, but this was solely for the education of the children of its employees. There was a parish school situated in the grounds and overseen by St Paul's Church. A school for boys and another for girls were also active at this time, but very little is known of their existence. There is sparse evidence of a further school controlled by two spinster sisters, but again nothing was recorded of the school's activities. There is documented proof of unofficial education in 'house schools' or adventure schools, at Hibernian Road and at Salem Street. October 1850 saw the adoption of the local government act. Two months later, in December, and a local administrative board had been created that eventually became the town council. This body of men were determined that the children of the town received every educational opportunity available to them; the enthusiasm with which this was enforced made the town one of the most educationally progressive in the northern region. The introduction of the Education Act in 1870 rapidly saw the publication of bylaws making school attendance compulsory for all children, which they did in temporary classrooms until permanent and adequate buildings became available. The first of these was a disused theatre in Drury Lane, the first of two Ellison Church of England schools opened in 1861, the second in 1882. St Bede's Infant School opened

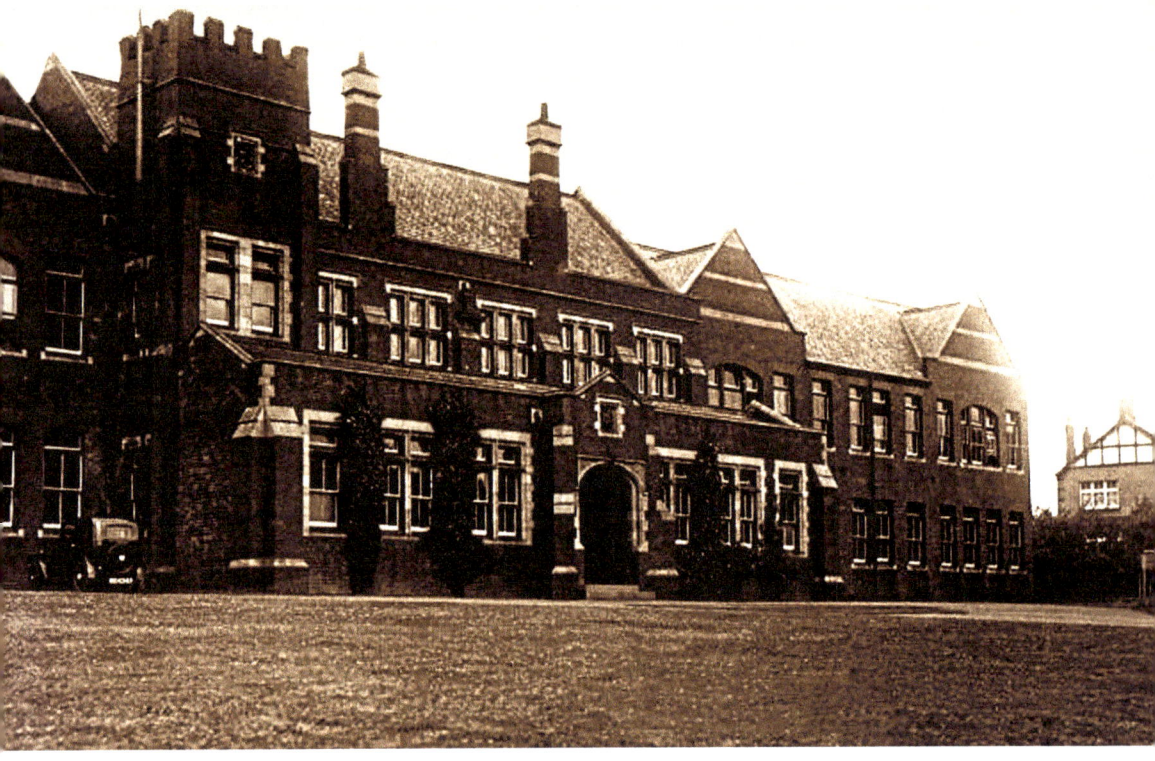

Jarrow Grammar School, 1938.

in 1868, and another for senior boys at Low Jarrow in 1872. The country's first board school, the Grange, opened in 1873, and later the same year Monkton National School opened, which became Bede Burn School. The year 1874 saw the opening of Dunn Street School and St Paul's National School in Chaytor Street, and Croft Terrace in 1894. In 1914, St Bede's in Harold Street opened, and in 1928 two houses in Pine Street were converted into Mayfield School for Girls. The enforcement of the compulsory education act, which also stated absenteeism will not be tolerated, was not agreeable to everyone. Generally, the people of Jarrow were poverty stricken at this particular time, to the extent that school fees could not be paid by some, and in extreme cases, the church paid the fees subject to each family's personal circumstances.

F

Football

Football has always been avidly played in Jarrow, whether in competition or a kick about in the back lanes. Schools were keen to organise inter-school competitions from the late Victorian period. The first team was St Bede's Hibernians, which was formed in 1890. From 1895 they won the coveted Sambotee Cup three years in succession. As the Hibernians went from strength to strength with no shortage of class players, a committee was formed in 1920 who appointed Bill Rice as chief coach. His expertise successfully led the team to many victories beginning with the coveted Palmer Memorial Cup in its first year under the direction of the committee, and winning every major trophy up until the outbreak of Second World War in 1939. The team was revived in 1950 after the war years and admitted to the South Shields and District League, which continued in providing an interest and recreation for younger members. The school boasted no shortage of players, as the most populated school in the area, giving it the advantage over neighbouring schools with in excess of 450 pupils from which to choose. In addition to this, the school had a perfectly good, well-tended

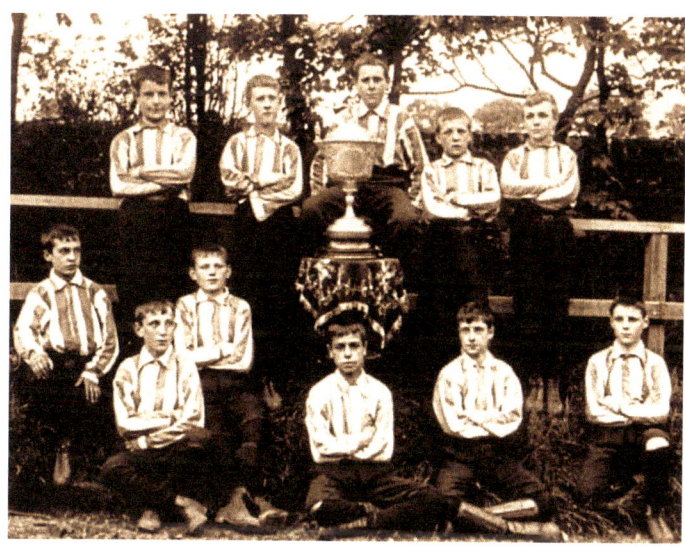

St Bede's Hibernians
Football Team from 1895.

football ground on its doorstep at Low Jarrow, and the team had the full support of the management committee and officials. On several occasions the team attracted publicity from the national press for its determination in reaching various cup finals, especially for its success in the second round of the Durham County Challenge Cup, when they were drawn against Bishop Auckland. No less than seventeen busloads of supporters travelled with the team, only to witness a 13-2 defeat. At half-time the team was losing by eight goals to nil, when one supporter caught the parish priest fumbling with his rosary, who commented to him 'It's a bit late for divine intervention Father'. 'No nothing of the sort,' replied the priest amusingly, 'I'm keeping the score.'

Food for Thought

Food and eating habits were to change dramatically during the 1960s. The small Italian community in Jarrow were more than familiar with pasta and how to cook it. However, it didn't take long for the trend of continental flavours to catch on. The first of the Jarrow shops to stock several varieties of dried pasta was, incidentally, the town's first self-service supermarket – Moore's in Bede Precinct – and it wasn't long before spaghetti bolognese became almost as popular as fish and chips. An upsurge in holiday packages to the Mediterranean was to further kick-start Britain's appetite for continental cuisine. Access to the ingredients for the preparation of these delicacies were becoming freely available at deli counters in most food stores. Closer to home, the nation's taste buds were dancing to the tune of Indian curry, which was rapidly growing in popularity. South Shields became the curry centre for the north-east region, with the first restaurant Anglo Asian opening in 1956, the premises of which are now occupied by Royal Tandoori restaurant in Ocean Road, specialising in Sylheti cuisine from the north-eastern region of Bangladesh.

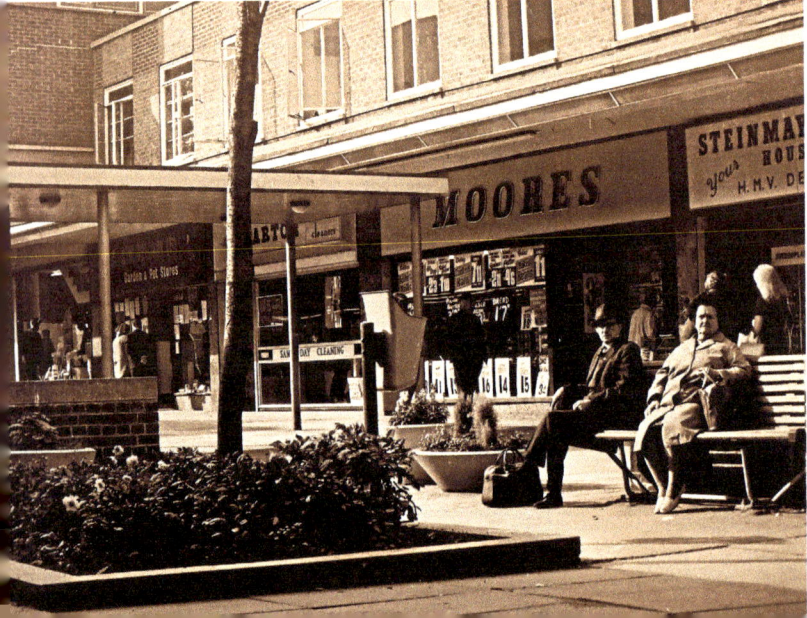

Moore's, Bede Precinct, the first self-service supermarket on Tyneside.

G

Gasworks

Since gas power was introduced in the British Isles over 200 years ago, gasholders – gasometers as they have become known – have been a distinctive but quite an ugly feature of town and city skylines up and down the country. It was William Murdoch who christened them gasometers after he invented gas lighting for our homes and thoroughfares in the nineteenth century. These storage tanks began to appear during the ensuing years and were used daily until recently, supplying the nation with gas when most houses and businesses were illuminated and heated with gas. The storage tanks at Curlew Road and at the Jarrow Gas Co. in Ferry Street, which once stored coal gas until the development of natural gas, were a reminder of how the town flourished in the shipyards and various other industries dependent on this type of fuel. The thriving gasworks located at the foot of Ferry Street was taken over by the South Shields Gas Co. around 1870, which was modified in 1876 and again in 1913, and employed many hundreds of men up until the 1960s. The gas industry has evolved with gas now stored in underground pipes and various facilities, making the eyesore gasholders across the country redundant and obsolete. In some rare cases it was necessary to conceal these tanks with brickwork structures resembling buildings.

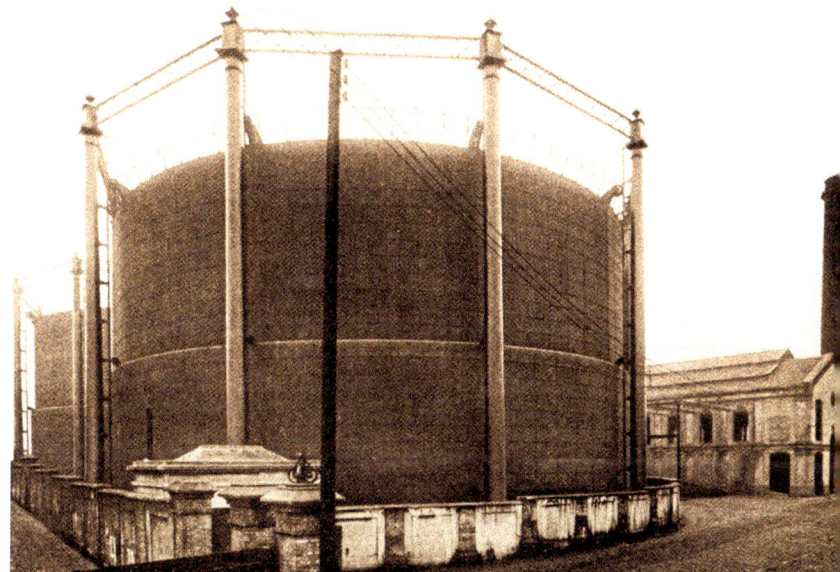

The gasworks in Ferry Street, 1920.

The National Grid Property is preserving several of the now disused gasholders in several ways in a bid to record and preserve a vital part of the country's industrial heritage. Part of this preservation programme incorporates partial regeneration of the structures in new developments, and donating artefacts to museums and schools. The Jarrow skyline improved dramatically as the last of these monstrosities in Curlew Road was removed piece by piece during 2017.

Gasworkers Social Club

As Palmer provided the Mechanics Institute in Ellison Street for his workforce, the gas authority provided a social club for its members of staff in Grange Road. The appointed manager was one of the town's colourful characters, Jimmy Mullen. One busy Saturday evening while serving behind the bar, he noticed a priest enter the room. Being of the Catholic faith, Jimmy recognised the difference between a priest and a vicar by the collar the man was wearing. 'Good Evening Father' Jimmy hailed across the room to the stranger, 'be with you in a moment'. Eventually the priest ordered half a pint of beer. 'On the house' Jimmy kindly said. Ten minutes later he poured him another beer, this time with a whisky chaser. After a while the bar became quiet, quiet enough to fill the clergyman's glass for the third time and promptly engage in conversation with him. 'Which parish are you from Father' enquired Jimmy, thinking he was the new curate from nearby St Bede's. 'I don't have a parish' came the reply. 'Well you must be a Missionary then'. 'No I'm not a Missionary either' said the stranger, finishing what was now his fifth glass of beer. At this the puzzled barman scratching his head enquired why he was dressed in cleric's clothes. The stranger gulped down another whisky chaser and helpfully replied, 'well I am at a fancy-dress party over the road at the Ex-servicemen's Club, and I only called in for a pint while

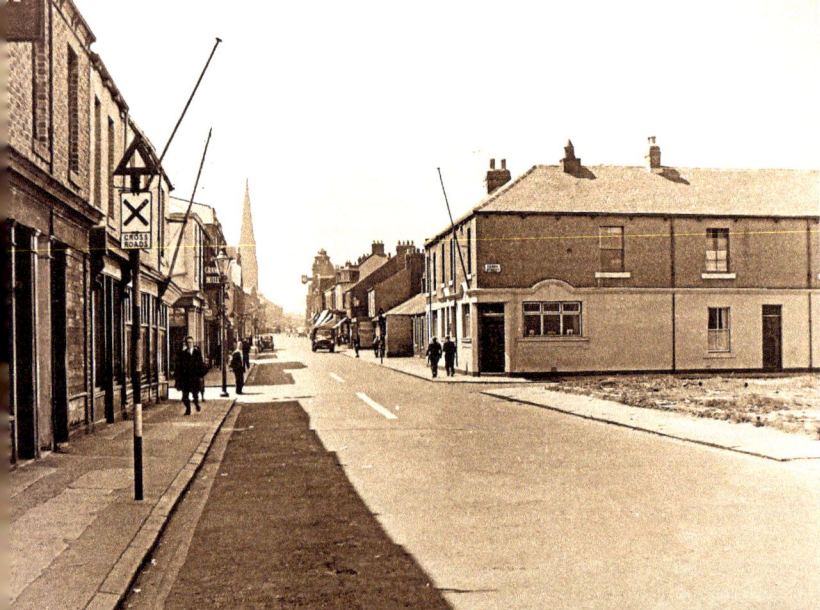

Grange Road from 1952 with Gas Workers Social Club (left) and Ex-servicemen's Club (right).

they were playing bingo, but thank you for your hospitality. Jimmy said nothing as the man left the bar. Apparently, this was the one and only time Jimmy was lost for words.

General Dealers

October 1954 saw food rationing abandoned in Jarrow. A typical breakfast of the time consisted of eggs, bacon and white bread, which was deemed a giant leap in the right direction after the long years of inferior produce and hardship during the Second World War. During the early 1950s, 60 per cent of working men in Jarrow returned home for lunch, which was considered the main meal of the day. Housewives shopped daily and did what they could with what little resources were available to them, and as comestibles were in such short supply, nothing was wasted; leftovers were always turned into another meal. The rare commodity of meat eaten at this time was mainly imported from South America, who charged extortionate prices for the privilege of supplying the nation with their second-rate produce. Eventually, the country refused to pay and sought another supplier. This action drastically reduced the meat ration to 5oz per person, per week. A small portion of butter and a reasonable amount of meat would most certainly have made a considerable difference to the family diet. To mark the coronation of HM Queen Elizabeth in 1953, the nation was given a public holiday, and households were given extra rations.

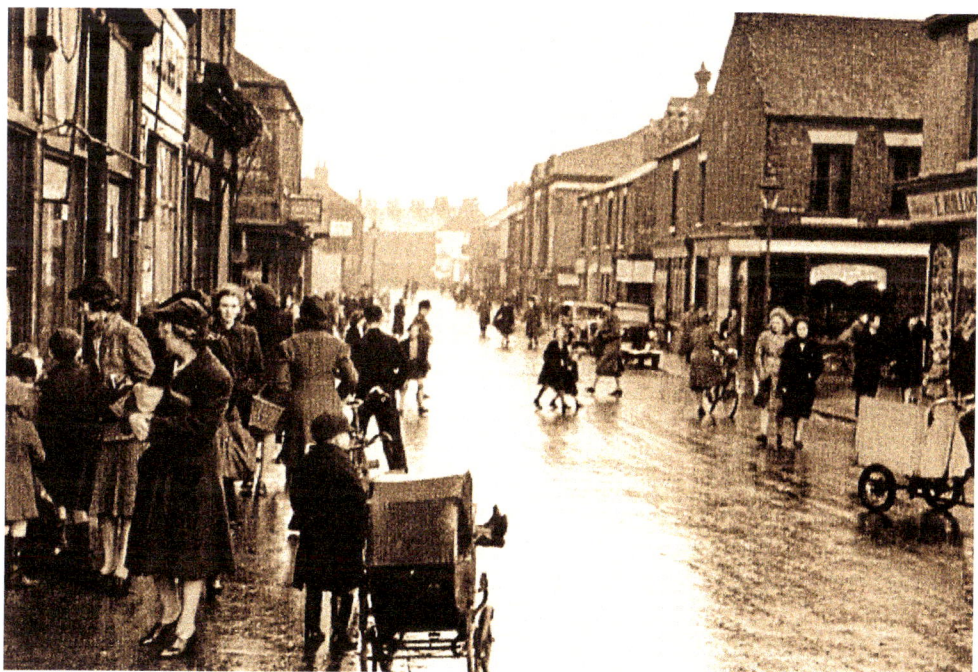

A busy Saturday morning in 1950s Grange Road.

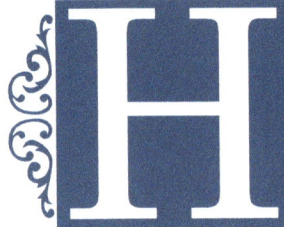

Housewives Choice

Being a housewife during the 1950s was most certainly a full-time job. Cooking, washing, shopping and generally keeping the house clean were laborious tasks without the modern conveniences we take for granted today. The cost of a refrigerator back then was prohibitively twelve times the average man's wage, and with only 5 per cent of the nation owning such a device. Around this time electrical retailers were beginning to pop up in the High Street nationwide. For Jarrow, Thomas and Richley in Ellison Street

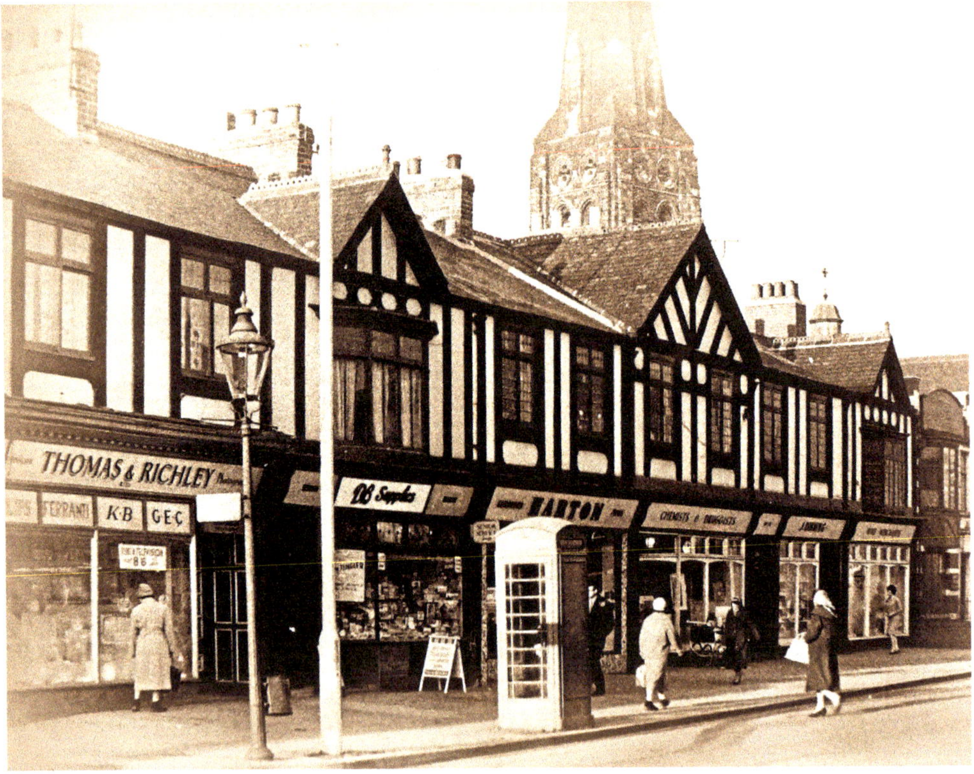

Ellison Street, 1955.

were the main retailers stocking domestic appliances. However, these must-have appliances were still very expensive, but the recent change in the law concerning hire purchase placed them within easy reach of those who could afford them, or could use them, as many houses in the town had not yet been converted to electricity.

Housing

A promise by the government for the provision of 250,000 new houses nationwide after the war was now taking shape. The mass demolition and rebuilding of these housing complexes progressed sufficiently enough for new towns to evolve almost overnight. For Jarrow, this promised a new beginning and would most certainly replace the deplorable living conditions endured by so many for so long. These modern new abodes had to be furnished, which was made possible with the relaxation of the utility restrictions in 1950. This contemporary desirable furniture was designed to substantially brighten up the modern dwellings. As the old property in Jarrow was torn down, the rag-and-bone men were busy combing the streets seeking out anything of value they could lay their hands on. High on their list of priorities was the now abundant supply of disused cast-iron fireplaces, which promised to be a valuable asset when sold to the scrap men in Pitt Street. Modern houses were now fitted with tiled and easy to clean modern alternatives to comply with the forthcoming Clean Air Act of 1956, or a 'smokeless zone' as it became known. This move meant domestic coal fires were banned from this time and an alternative fuel had to be sourced. This came in the form of coke and anthracite, both of which burned slowly with a cosy glow, and without the harmful gasses of other fuels.

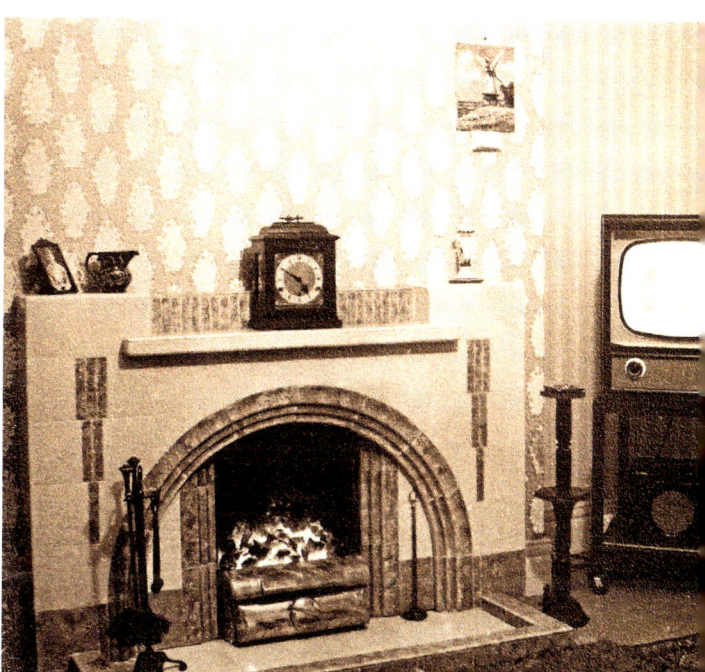

Modern housing at Primrose, 1955.

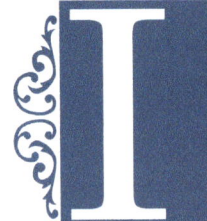

Isolation Hospital

Because of the welcome increase in trade on the River Tyne, and with increasing volumes of traffic of vessels of varying capacities arriving daily, some laden with cargo while others for repair, concerns were growing for the safety of the workforce in the busy river ports. In the nineteenth century, the Port of Tyne Sanitary Authority realised the requirement of quarantine facilities was paramount, possibly isolated from the mainland, which could be the solution to the prevention of infectious disease. The idea of a floating hospital emerged, and by 1885 building work commenced. The successful launch of the hospital came about on 2 August 1886 and moored into position at Jarrow close to the 'slake'. The facility offered care and treatment for seamen from foreign parts suffering from rare and infectious diseases contracted abroad. It was thought the hospital would contain such diseases and reduce the risk of contamination with people residing either side of the river. It became the practice and eventually an obligation for vessels entering the Tyne to display a yellow pennant signifying it was arriving from foreign waters.

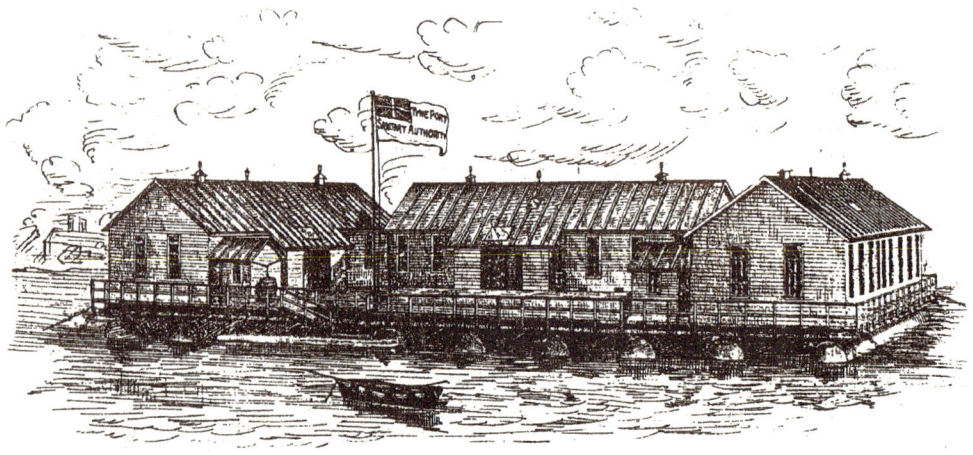

Quarantine and Isolation Hospital moored in the Tyne from 1886 to 1920.

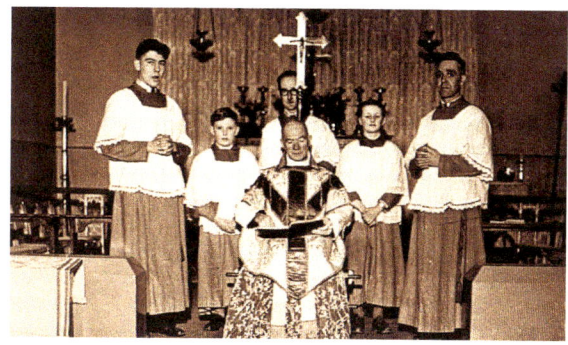

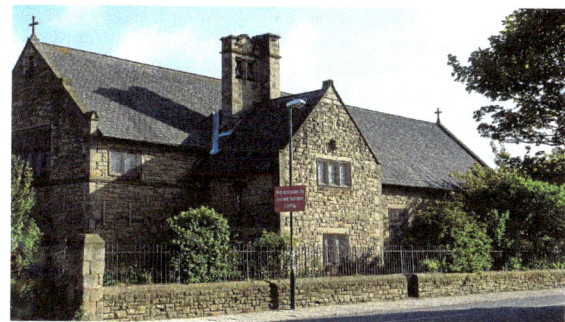

Revd Wallace and altar servers, 1940,
and St Mark's Church, Salem Street.

Isabella Drewett Brown

Isabella Drewett Brown, widow of the late Thomas Drewett Brown, who owned a considerable amount of land at Jarrow, passed away in 1894. Although she resided at Croft, North Yorkshire, she was interred at St Paul's churchyard at her family's request. Among the many gifts she bequeathed to the town was the total cost of the building of St Peter's Church at Ferry Street, and the land upon which St Mark's Church was built along with a donation of £1,000. The church was consecrated in 1896 by the Bishop of Durham Revd Dr Hornby. It was built with stone quarried at Hebburn at a cost of £2.500. The 300-seat church was used as a chapel of ease for St Paul's Church. Prior to the erection of the building the congregation worshipped at the Mission Hall in High Street. The building was completed on time in 1895, but consecration was delayed because of a deficit of a final payment of £400. Friends of the church covered this shortfall, which paved the way for the consecration.

Industry

Jarrow has been associated with industry since the seventh century and the time of Venerable Bede, when coloured glass was manufactured close to the Benedictine monastery along with metalwork and, although somewhat primitive, a facility for tanning hides. During

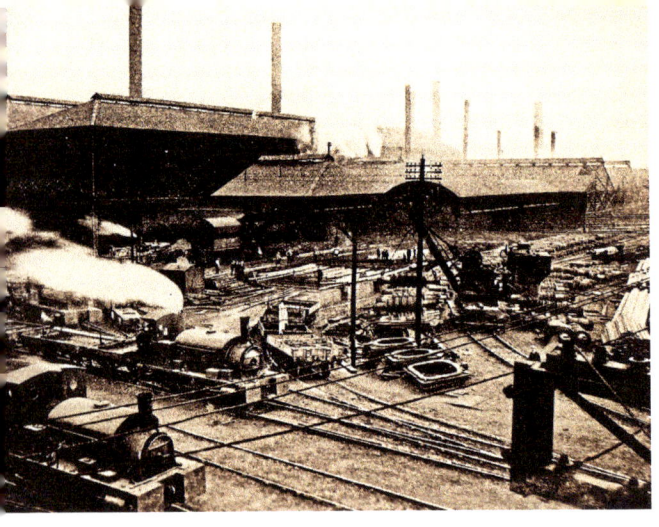

Palmers' Shipyard in full production, 1912.

the fourteenth and fifteenth centuries, rope and sail making were prolific close to the river embankment along with salt winning, produced from the mineral rich waters of the North Sea. There is also evidence at Durham Cathedral of coal mining in the region from as early as 1618; this is highly probable because of the town's proximity to the sea and the easily recoverable coal beneath it. However, it was Simon Temple who was responsible for mining coal commercially. In 1803, he discovered a coal seam that eventually evolved into the infamous Alfred Pit. The coal it produced was being shipped to the south of the country just as fast as it was being surfaced, thus commencing the industrial growth of Jarrow. The successful manufacture of quality paper from a mill at Springwell began around 1840. The manufacture of chemicals commenced in 1845 by Jefferson's on land close to Quay Corner. The chemical industry was to flourish in this part of town as two more companies were attracted to it – Kenmires and Richardson's. Foreign competition and a crippling global recession in the manufacturing process of chemicals forced the industry away from Jarrow during the 1930s. However, it was resurrected in 1954 at the arrival of American giants Charles Lennig & Co. As the River Tyne flourished with traffic coming and going, the need for a shipyard solely for the repair of the many vessels that were now passing this way became evident. The Mercantile Dry Dock & Engineering Co. filled this position in 1885 with a single dry dock. The latter part of the nineteenth and twentieth centuries saw a fairly stable and hopeful period with a sustained, if irregular, assortment of colliers, tankers and cargo boats on this busy waterway, which was answering to the demands of industry for the import and export of produce.

Italian Job

Towards the end of the nineteenth and the beginning of the twentieth centuries, there was rather a large influx of southern Italian immigrants seeking work and hoping to settle in north-east England. Many arrived penniless and with few belongings and even fewer prospects. The arduous two-week-long journey from Italy was almost always by train, travelling third class sitting and sleeping on hard wooden benches, surviving solely on what provisions they had brought with them, generally a diet of hard boiled eggs, vegetables and bread. Jarrow was to become home to a moderate proportion of the immigrants including my own grandmother Rosa Risi, together with her nieces and nephews. They recognised the absence of ice-cream parlours, and with what resources and little funds that were available to them, they grasped the opportunity to invest in a business, hard work and determination resulting in a superior lifestyle in England than what their mother country offered. Eventually my grandmother's nieces and nephews relocated to Edinburgh in Scotland, and similar to their time in Jarrow, worked extremely hard and enjoyed the trappings successful businesses bring. Another of the immigrant families to enjoy moderate success was Salvatore Rea and his wife Martha, originally from Arpino in southern Italy, who arrived in Middlesbrough in 1898, where they resided for a period of seven years. After a further year in Newcastle they decided Jarrow was where they wanted to make their living purveying ice cream, which they did for many years up until the 1960s. In an unlikely combination of business interests Salvatore, assisted by his son Dominic and while operating a successful ice-cream parlour, decided to invest in a demolition business until 1960, when he pursued a career in road haulage.

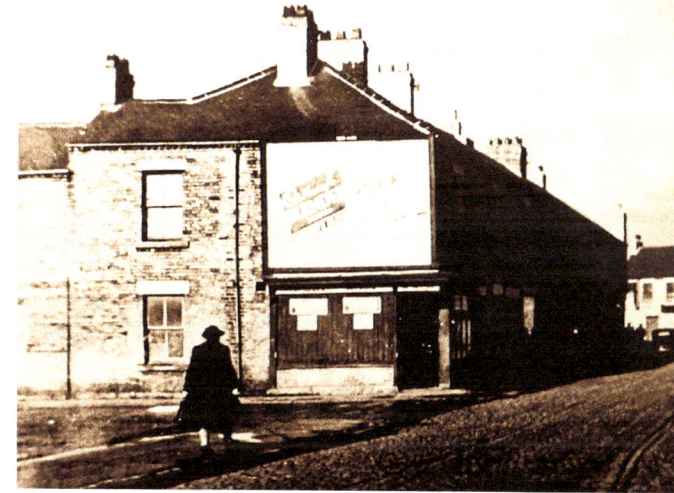

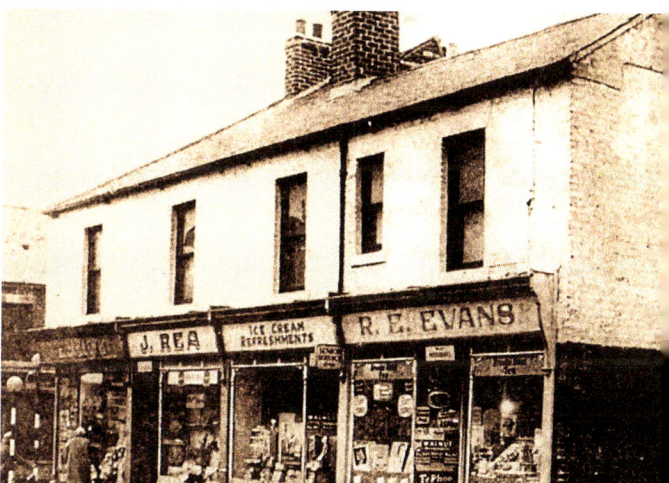

Mrs Risi's and J. Rea's ice-cream parlours, in Staple Road and Grange Road respectively, in 1950.

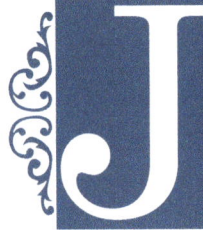

Joseph Bede Symonds

Born in Jarrow in 1900, Joseph Bede Symonds was one of a family of twenty-one children. After serving in the army as a sergeant-major in the Royal Highland Regiment of the Black Watch in India, on his return to Jarrow he married Lavinia Harrison with whom he fathered thirteen children. A prominent figure in the organisation of the 1936 Jarrow Crusade, Symonds held many important and prestigious offices throughout his illustrious career. After his successful campaign for councillor for the Labour Party, he rapidly rose to the position of alderman for the Borough of Jarrow. In 1945, he was elected mayor of the town with an overwhelming majority, and later chairman of the National Housing Committee. He was headstrong and a major influence in the construction of the Tyne Pedestrian Tunnel. He strongly opposed a proposition to build a bridge spanning the river, construction of which would have created the demolition of several perfectly sound council houses. Symonds relocated to Whitehaven in Cumberland and was elected Member of Parliament for the town in 1959, holding the position until his retirement in 1970. He was awarded the Order of the British Empire for services to the disabled, and became a national authority on municipal housing.

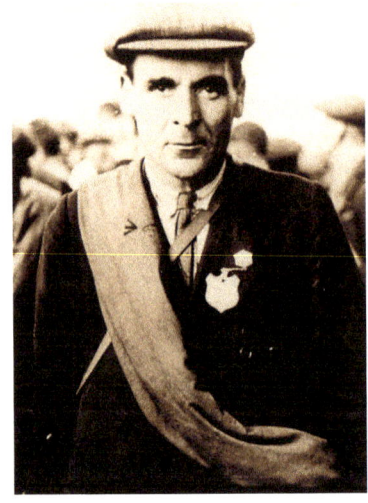

Alderman Joseph Bede Symonds, stalwart of the Jarrow Crusade.

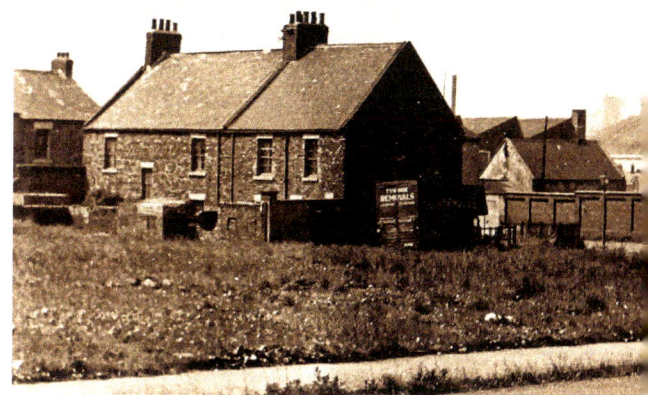

James Hunter Carr's residence and mushroom farm at Tyne Street, 1952.

James Hunter Carr

I first met James Hunter Carr in 1962 just after I left school and was working as an apprentice photographer. Even at this very young age I realised I was in the company of a very clever man. I recall he was quite tall, extremely well dressed in a crisp white shirt, black suit and wearing a homburg. Working from a terraced house in Tyne Street, James Hunter Carr earned his living as a mushroom farmer selling his produce to local fruit and vegetable retailers. He was also a qualified musician in both teaching and composing, and a mathematician, scientist and photographer. He was an accomplished author penning the *Sulphur Cough* in 1952 and in 1964 he wrote a comprehensive scientific theology, heavily influenced by his fascination for Swedish scientist and philosopher Emanuel Svedberg, entitled *Introduction to the Science of Correspondences.* Hunter Carr invented a system enabling him to produce perfume from whale oil, but in the interests of health and safety was not permitted to market the invention on the grounds of it being environmentally unfriendly. His vast knowledge of electronics and radio frequencies contributed a small but important role in the invention of radar. He was often referred to as a genius, but the modest bachelor was always less than comfortable with the accolade. James Hunter Carr photographed many aspects of Jarrow with a simple camera recording streets, notable buildings and habits of the people during the 1940s and '50s, compiling a detailed photographic record of the town. He took particular interest in the region of the slake taking a series of images in order to produce a single panoramic study of the area. This legacy of photographs, complete with negatives and technical details, were produced for his personal entertainment and never published. Like many buildings in Jarrow around 1960, Hunter Carr's property was greatly in need of attention, and by 1963 he took up residence at the Kent Hotel in Jesmond. He passed away soon after his relocation. It was my good fortune to inherit Hunter Carr's voluminous collection of images around 1967, and again I take pleasure in sharing a selection of them with you through these pages.

Jarrow Instruction Centre

The Jarrow Instruction Centre (JIC) was created during the dark days of the depression to help unemployed men channel their energies into something worthwhile. In 1933, a football league comprising twenty-four teams was created. The boots strips and

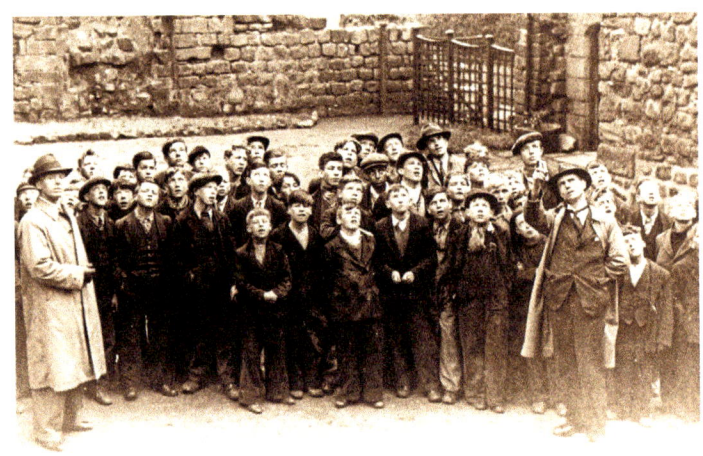

Jarrow Instruction Centre organisers with boy's club at the monastery ruins, 1935.

accessories were supplied by readers of *The Times* newspaper and Surrey sportsmen. Because of this act of generosity just a small amount of money was required from the Surrey Fund, enabling it to be used for more worthwhile causes. This league proved to be most successful and attracted huge crowds to every game. Two thousand spectators attended the final at Campbell Park ground, at which Sir John Jarvis 'kicked off' and presented the trophy. Around this time, the non-footballing men were encouraged to return to physical exercise with council assistance, who granted permission for the public baths in Walter Street to be used as a gymnasium. No fewer than 4,000 attendees were recorded, which created the welcome need for extra sessions to accommodate the fitness fanatics. The council requested that during the summer months the baths be used for what they were intended, and the group was asked to continue their physical fitness at the Drill Hall, where training would continue in and out doors. A boxing section was flourishing as was the formation of a rugby football club. These activities were under the watchful eye of Lt-Commander Melville R. N., acting sports organiser for Jarrow Instruction Centre. The young people of the town were not forgotten. The interest shown by HRH George V resulted in the introduction of his personal secretary, Commander Adams, to Sir John Jarvis. This resulted in a special grant for the commencement of a boys' club in Jarrow in conjunction with the Durham County Association of Boys Clubs. The former police station in High Street was thought the ideal venue for such an enterprise. The nominal rent was attractive enough for the project to go ahead. The materials for decoration were provided with a grant of £500 from His Majesty George V. Among the girls' activities were dressmaking, a choral society and folk dancing.

Jarrow Gibbet

During the infamous Northumberland and Durham miners' great strike of 1832, Jarrow had its own troubles to contend with: not only did the town's mining fraternity

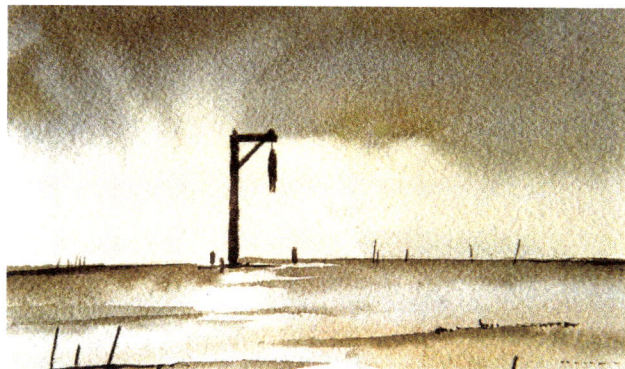

The Jarrow Gibbet from 1832.

take part in the coal war, causing extreme hardship, but two wayward drunken Jarrow pitmen accosted a well-known and respected local businessman and Justice of the Peace, Nicholas Fairles. On June 11, Fairles was riding on horseback close to Tyne Dock when he was stopped, assaulted and robbed by William Jobling and Ralph Armstrong. Fairles was so severely injured that the seventy-one-year-old magistrate died of his injuries ten days later on 21 June. Warrants were issued for the arrest of the two pitmen, resulting in the capture of Jobling, who was charged with murder; however, it is generally thought Armstrong made his escape to Australia. Jobling was tried at Durham Assizes on 1 August; the jury took just fifteen minutes to reach a guilty verdict and condemned the pitman to death. He was executed on 3 August 1832. Three days later, his body was taken to Jarrow Slake on a flat-top horse-drawn wagon flanked by soldiers, covered with pitch and clamped in an iron cage. A 22-foot-high gibbet was erected on the Slake close to the site of the attack and Jobling's caged body suspended from it, and remained this way for all to see as a reminder to the villains of the parish that these acts of brutality will not be tolerated. On the night of the 31 August, the body mysteriously disappeared. Many theories have been offered as to its disappearance, the most probable being the body was removed and buried in the Tyne. Jobling's widow Isabella never recovered from the atrocity and passed away peacefully in senility at a workhouse in South Shields in 1890.

Jarrow Crusade

Much has been documented and lamented about the Jarrow Crusade to London in 1936 and the technicalities of how and why it came about. It was a political demonstration for jobs and the right to work, and not, as the majority of the nation's press reported, a 'hunger march'. Torrential rain greeted the men on their arrival to the capital, and as predicted officialdom at Parliament was most unsympathetic as the Conservative government totally disapproved of the demonstration and abruptly declined the contingent a hearing. An appeal by Labour Party Leader Clement Attlee, on the grounds that the 'crusaders' reserved the right to approach Parliament for assistance,

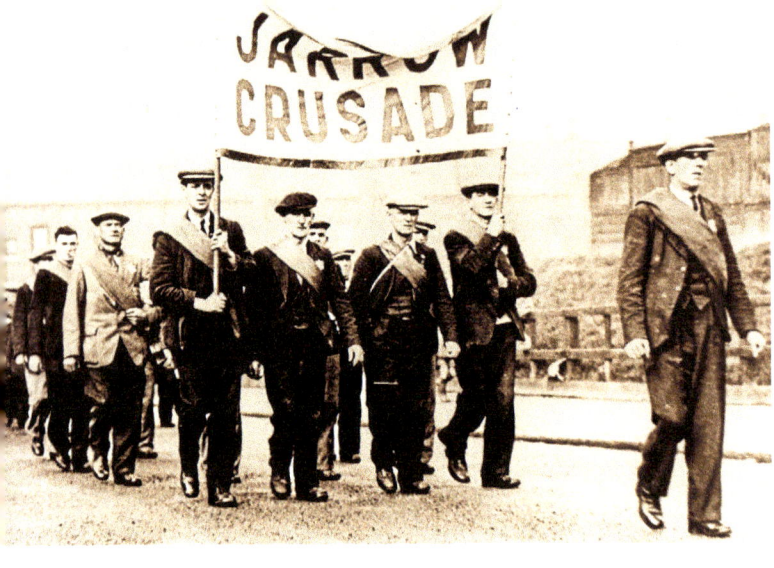

Jarrow Crusade passing through Huddersfield, 1936.

was also rejected. Eventually, the government relented and a petition, supported by 10,000 signatures, the men carried the 300 miles to London was eventually deposited by Jarrow MP Ellen Wilkinson, who reminded the house that formerly 10,000 men, women and boys were employed in the town, but today the figure resembles 100. The problem of constitutional rights reared its head, but yet again the government refused to back down, with the retort 'all grievances should be directed through the appropriate channels to Parliament'. Further coverage by the media, only this time they got it right: 'the men returned to Jarrow, to the street corners, bewildered and downhearted at the Government's arrogant and determined refusal of assistance'.

Jarrow Metal Industries

Hope and prosperity was to sail into Jarrow in 1938 in the form of SS *Berengaria*. The vessel was to be broken up at Jarrow providing months of work for hundreds of unemployed men from the town as part of the John Jarvis Initiative. Prior to the commencement of the work, Sir John invited the mayor and local dignitaries on board the crippled vessel for a reception and a very welcome announcement of two new industries to Jarrow: The Jarrow metal industry, and Jarrow tube works.

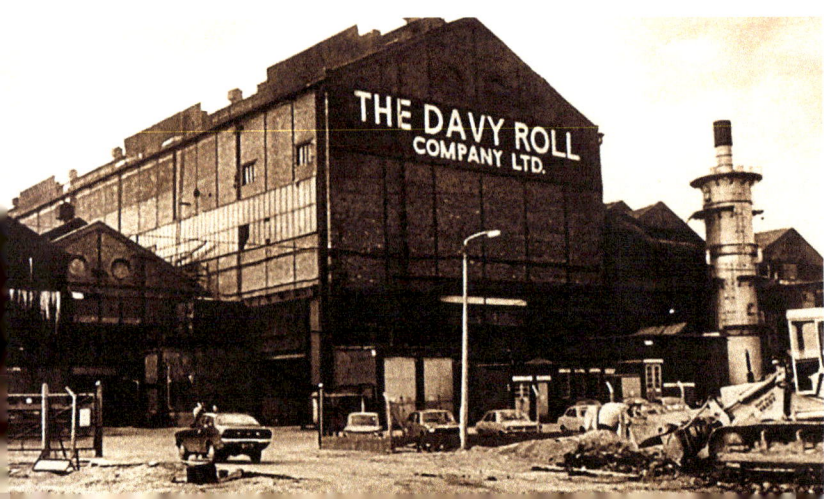

Jarrow metal industries, 1969.

Sir John delivered an address that paid tribute to the Venerable Bede and the town council, following this with telegrams of good wishes from his Majesty Edward VII and Prime Minister Neville Chamberlain on behalf of the government. The Duchess of Northumberland Helen Percy performed the official opening ceremony. The event was concluded with a lavish luncheon at Newcastle's Old Assembly Rooms, when a toast was proposed by Jarvis to His Majesty the King, and to the chairman of the committee, the presiding Mayor of Jarrow Alderman Terence O'Connor.

Jarrow Slake

The Saxon word 'Gyrwy', long since corrupted into Jarrow, translated means 'marsh or fen', and it was from this translation the town took its name. The expanse of water known as the 'slake', which it has been referred to for centuries, is nothing more than a corruption of the term 'Jarrow's Lake'. On a number separate occasions centuries apart the 'slake' was used: by the Romans to anchor their vessels at the mouth of the River Don and by King Egfrid to shelter the whole of his fleet from the savage northern winter, and again by the plundering Danes. The 'slake' itself was an extensive wasteland estimated to have occupied an area of 1,000 acres, covered with water from the spring tides. Close to this former barren land was a scattering of country houses. The first Jarrow Hall, home of Simon Temple on Church Bank, another Jarrow Lodge on the southern edge of the 'slake', was the home of antiquarian and devoted ornithologist John Straker, where he housed a museum containing at least one of each species of migratory and native birds that frequented the area. Perhaps the most imposing of these residences was Simonside Hall, home to magistrate Henry Major, which commanded splendid views of the River Tyne and neighbouring countryside. In more recent times this sheltered basin was used for maturing timbers.

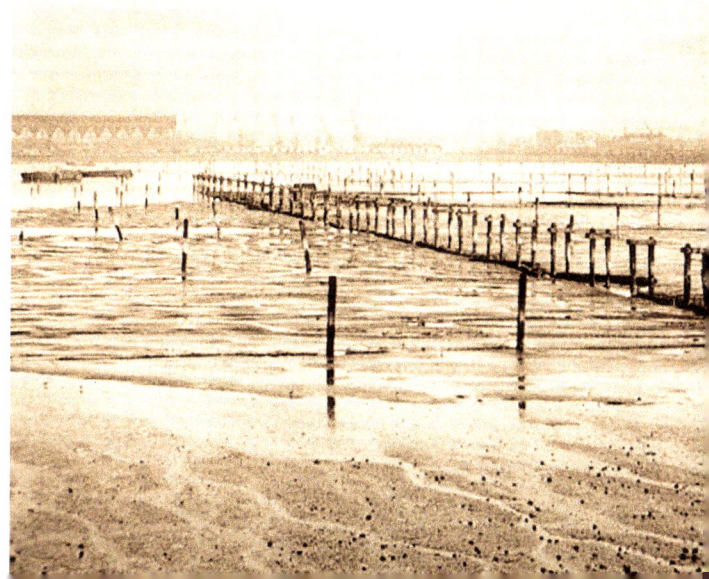

Jarrow slake and timber ponds, 1950.

John Miles

John Miles was born the second son to Alec and Doris Errington at Stead Street in the town in 1949. John commenced his education at St Peter's school in the town and after passing the eleven plus exam, concluded at Jarrow Grammar School. From a very early age he showed and developed an interest in music, often playing on his father's piano, which encouraged his parents to send him for piano lessons. Soon John's attention turned towards the guitar and a programme of expert tuition at nearby Hebburn. It was his music teacher at Grammar School, Jimmy Joseph, who further encouraged John to seek a career in music. A series of small-time bands were to provide the stepping stones for the musicians glittering career: initially The Derringers, The New Atlantians and later The Urge, playing regularly at local nightspots, and with Paul Thompson in a band called The Influence. Paul later found fame with Roxy Music. While appearing at Peter Stringfellow's nightspot in Leeds, and with time on his hands one Saturday afternoon in 1972 – just prior to his marriage to childhood sweetheart Eileen – John casually played the piano. He recorded forty minutes of music in different styles, which was eventually edited down to six minutes. Little did he know at the time, but this important six minutes was to change his life. Encouraged by what he was listening to, he decided to write lyrics to go with it. 'Music Was My First Love' was born in a tiny guest house in Leeds. The song was recorded in 1975 but not released until the following year. Tipped to be a number one hit, it was beaten to the top spot by Brotherhood of Man, who had recently won the Eurovision Song Contest, with 'Save Your Kisses for Me'. Alas 'Music' didn't reach the number one slot, but John did receive the coveted Ivor Novello Award for his composition in 1977. In 1986, John was invited to Los Angeles to audition for Tina Turner's band, who was impressed with his style and what the musician had to offer, and promptly offered him the position, which took him on seven worldwide tours. This was followed by a two-year tour with Joe Cocker playing guitar and keyboard, and singing with Jimmy Page on the Outrider tour in 1988. A remarkable and dazzling career for another of Jarrow's famous sons.

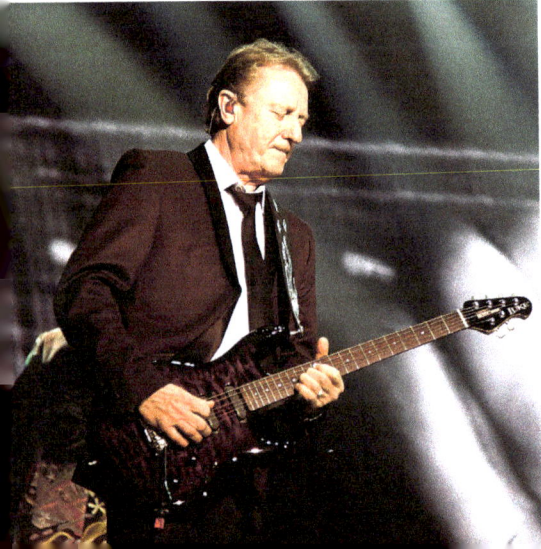

Rock star and composer John Miles.

K

Kino Theatre

The Kino Theatre was located in Grange Road in a former washhouse and furniture warehouse. The premises were converted into the theatre in 1908. However, it was closed to the public for renovation two years later in 1910. The building was extended and refurbished to accommodate and seat in excess of 1,000 patrons. The New Kino Theatre opened in August the same year. The owner of the theatre, entrepreneur Dixon Scott, invested huge amounts of capital in the latest projection equipment and sound systems available. A further name change for the popular cinema came about in 1929, when it was renamed The Regal Theatre, and eventually the Regal. As a trip to the flicks was rapidly losing popularity to television, the cinema closed in 1960, reopening as the Crown Bingo Club in 1961. In 1972, the Noble Organisation took over the day-to-day running of the club, reverting it back to its original use to that of a cinema, as the popular pastime made a comeback. Failing to make the company's predicted targets, it once again reverted to a bingo hall. As the game lost popularity, the building was subsequently demolished in 1983.

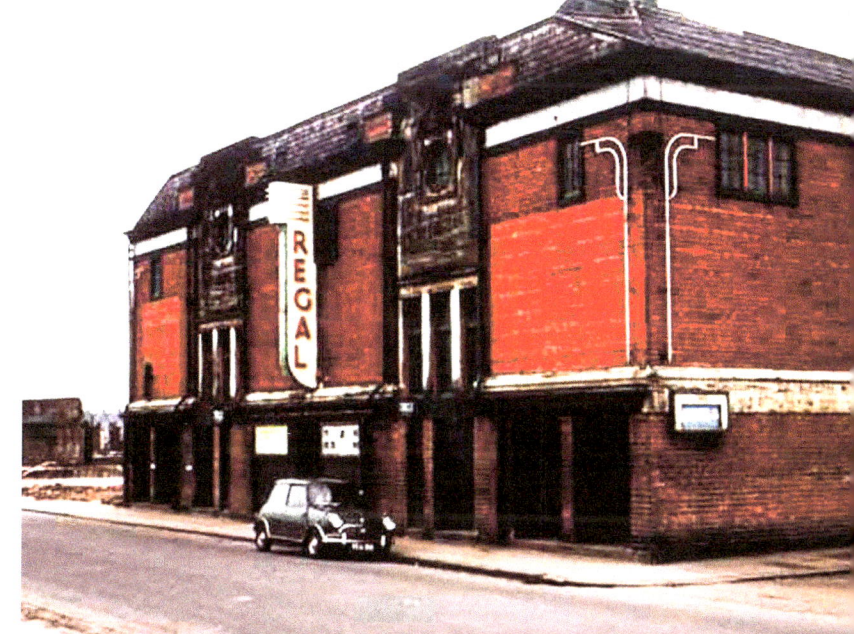

Former Kino Theatre in Grange Road, 1963.

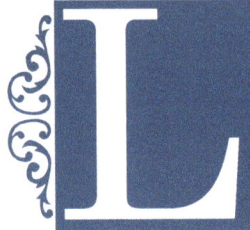

Lord Don Dixon

Born in 1929 at Caledonian Road, Jarrow, Donald, eldest son of Albert and Jane Dixon, was educated at Ellison Secondary Modern School in the town from 1934 to 1943. Leaving school aged fourteen; Don sought a career in the shipyards as a shipwright. Upon completion of his apprenticeship, he served two years national service in HM Forces, spending much of the time abroad. Returning to Jarrow and his profession, he became the voice of his fellow workers as representative for the GMB Union where he was respected by management and the workforce for his no nonsense approach. He served the town as councillor for several years, and was elected Mayor of Jarrow in 1971, and awarded Freeman of the Borough. Two years later in 1973, the metropolitan borough of South Tyneside was in the process of being formed, which included South Shields, the Borough of Jarrow, and urban districts of Hebburn and Boldon.

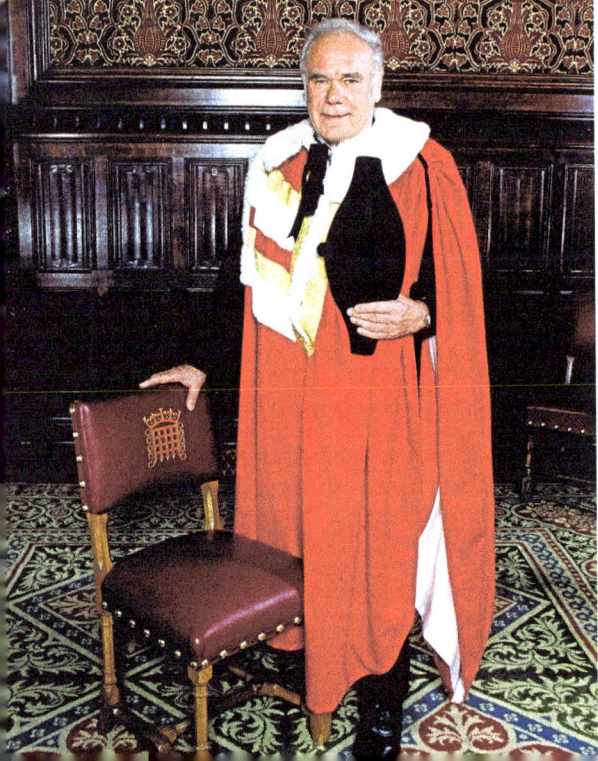

The Right Honourable Lord Don Dixon D. L.

L

After the completion of the borough in 1974, Councillor Dixon served as chairman of the housing committee. Don married Doreen Hall in 1979, and the same year he was raised to the position of Member of Parliament for Jarrow, relieving retiring MP Ernest Fernyhough of his duties, a position which he held from 1947. He was appointed to the Whips Office by Neil Kinnock in 1983, and his Parliamentary activities elevated him to the position of Deputy Chief Whip in 1987. The highly thought of MP was renowned for his honesty and directness in the House of Commons. John Major requested that Tony Blair recommended Don to the Privy Council for the responsible position of Privy Councillor. The same year, he was accepted to the house as life peer Donald Baron Dixon in 1997, after his resignation from the House of Commons. Trusted friend and former Jarrow Councillor George Porter was the Baron's Parliamentary Assistant from 1989. In 2016, Lord Dixon tended his resignation to the house on the grounds of health issues. After a long and illustrious life and career in politics, Donald Baron Dixon passed away in February 2017 aged eighty-seven.

Leo Connolly

Jarrow, for close to 200 years, has had a fond association with Ireland ever since an influx of our Irish cousins settled here in the town, which was at that particular time hovering over the brink of it becoming a boom town due to the advent of our lucrative modern shipbuilding industry. Peter Lally came from Connemara Co. Galway in the west of the Emerald Isle seeking work, and settled here in 1910 aged nineteen. He met

Irish tenor and gentleman Leo Connolly.

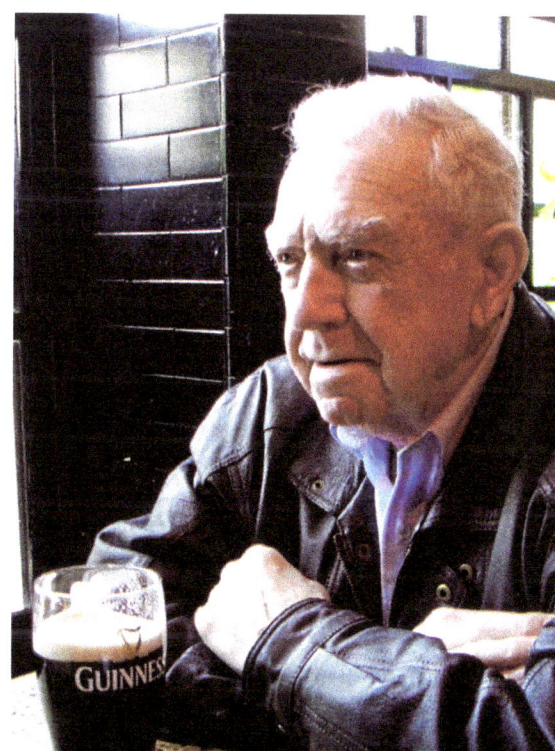

his beloved Elizabeth, and they were married at St Bede's Church in 1917 and reared three daughters. Leo Jr was born in Nixon Street in 1929, and from the age of twelve he was raised with his three sisters at the Commercial Hotel in Commercial Road. Leo, the only son of Leo and Barbara, was educated at St Bede's School in the town, where he began singing in the school choir at a very young age. Upon leaving school Leo worked as a shipwright in the Tyne yards, and entertained locally until he was called for national service. He was posted to Egypt towards the end of the Second World War to keep guard over the Italian and German prisoners who he entertained while they awaited repatriation. Upon the tenor's return to Jarrow, the golden tones of one of the town's most memorable sons were once again heard and echoed for miles around as he entertained thousands at Ceilidhs and Irish-themed evenings in the region's countless social clubs. He married his sweetheart Sheila Mullen in 1952 and reared two daughters, Maureen and Angelina. So very proud of his Irish ancestry, one of the easy-listening maestro's greatest achievements, who deemed it a great honour and a privilege, was being chosen to sing for the former Irish President Mary Mc Aleese at the Tyneside Irish Festival in 2003. He also sang for the Prince of Wales and the Duke of Cumberland, and several more well-known public houses. The jovial Irishman recorded and released a successful CD, *The Connolly Collection,* during the 1990s. Sadly, Leo passed away in July 2015 soon after his final trip to the land of his forefathers, his beloved County Galway.

Lambs Potato Crisps

The invention of the potato crisp came about quite by accident in America in 1853, as a cook tried to please an irate customer who complained his French fries were too thick. Slicing the potato ultra thin, the cook George Crum fried and salted them, resulting in the potato chip. To his amazement, the customer Cornelius Vanderbilt

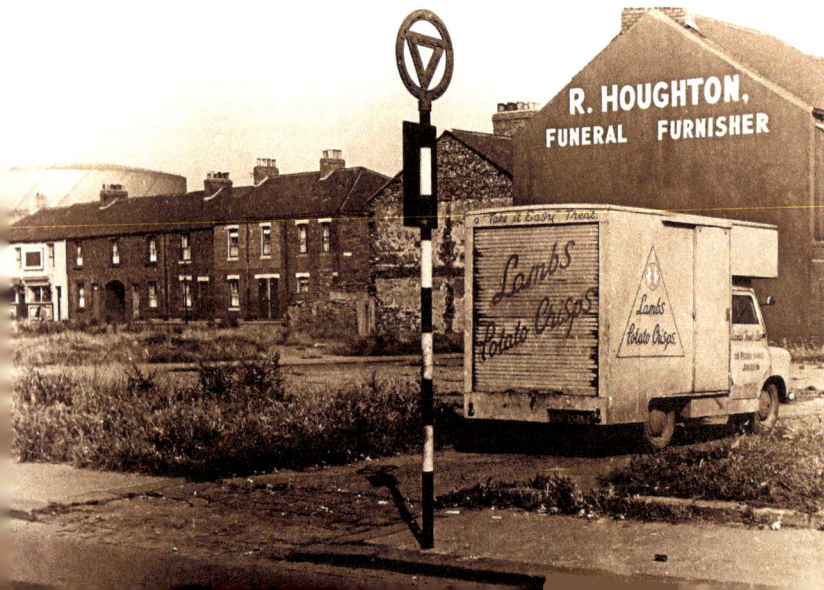

Lambs potato crisps delivery van parked at Ferry Street, 1954.

loved them. Today the potato crisp plays a dominant role in the snack food industry, which is dominated by Walkers with around 60 per cent of the market. Lambs snack foods were founded in 1937 at a small factory in Birtley manufacturing potato crisps. Because of the high demand for the popular snack, larger premises were sought. A site in Jarrow was purchased and by 1949 the building in Ferry Street was converted. The factory was equipped with the most up-to-date machinery so that during the cooking and packaging of the crisps they are untouched by hand. Lambs' output rose to in excess of 30 per cent to that of the former factory in Birtley. A process was developed at the factory monitoring potato quality, making this one of the most efficient plants in the country. As the business went from strength to strength, the need for a warehouse became necessary. Premises in nearby Staple Road were utilised until Tudor Foods Ltd purchased the company in 1959, when the land was required by the council for a housing development.

London & Newcastle Tea Co.

Shopping in Jarrow today is a very different experience than it was in the past, during times of high unemployment, depression and the anxiety of what the future held. A shopping list from days gone by certainly makes interesting reading. Totally devoid of processed food, it consisted mainly of store cupboard basics such as bacon, cheese, apples, lard and bread, all which were available from the L & N, which was the trading name for one of the country's leading grocers, London & Newcastle Tea Co., who specialised in – as the name suggests – tea and groceries and offered customers tokens and stamps that could be redeemed for gifts. The company was dissolved during the 1960s, and from then traded under the banner of Fine Fare Ltd. Occasionally, the thrifty housewife would manage to save enough money from the

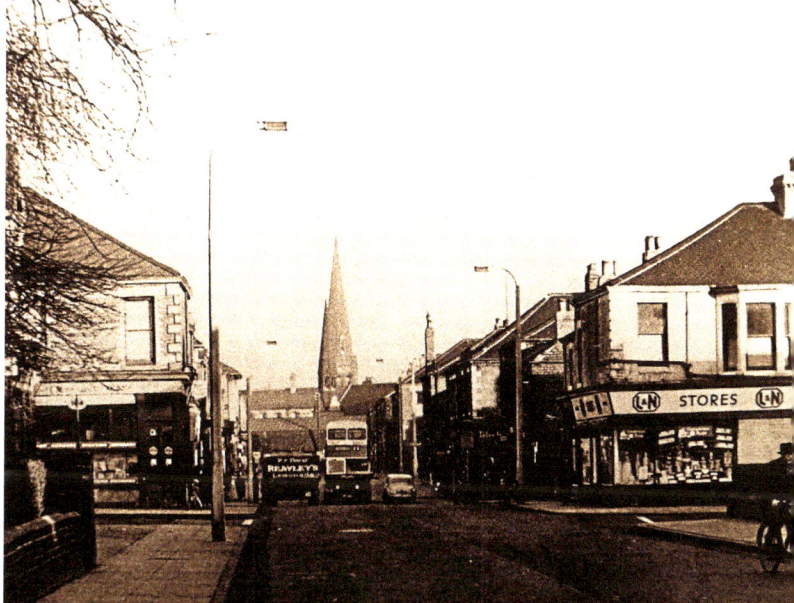

London & Newcastle Tea Co., Bede Burn Road, 1952.

weekly grocery budget to purchase a tin of salmon perhaps once a month. Meal times were often supplemented with produce from the many allotments located at Pigsty Avenue at the foot of the cemetery bank. Sunday afternoons were generally put to one side for baking things such as suet puddings, bread, tarts and scones ready in time for tea – careful housewives could make a stone of flour go a very long way. Candles were nearly always high on the shopping list as houses were without electricity, with gas being the sole source of energy for lighting and cooking for those who could afford it. The alternative was huge pans of water simmering gently over an open fire, which was used for cooking, brewing tea and washing. Among items missing from a modern-day shopping list would be dolly blue, a clothes whitener, an enormous bar of washing soap used specifically for the laundry, and rubby stone, a chalk-like substance used primarily for cleaning the front step. Times were very hard during the 1930s and '40s but people managed with what they had and what was available to them.

Lamplighters

Lamplighters in Jarrow were to disappear from our streets after the introduction of electricity in the early years of the twentieth century. In February 1900, a special meeting was called at the Corporation offices to discuss the introduction of electric light, both in our streets and homes. It was moved that the County of Durham Distribution Co. was to be entrusted with the illumination of our neighbourhood. The price of the power offered was extremely favourable at 7*d* per unit for the first 100 hours per quarter and 1*d* per unit for subsequent hours – these rates fought off all serious competition. However, it was only the principal streets and thoroughfares that were to enjoy the benefits of electricity. Gaslight was to remain as the prime source of street lighting. As the illumination of the lights became automated during the 1950s, the lamplighter's duties were simply to maintain them.

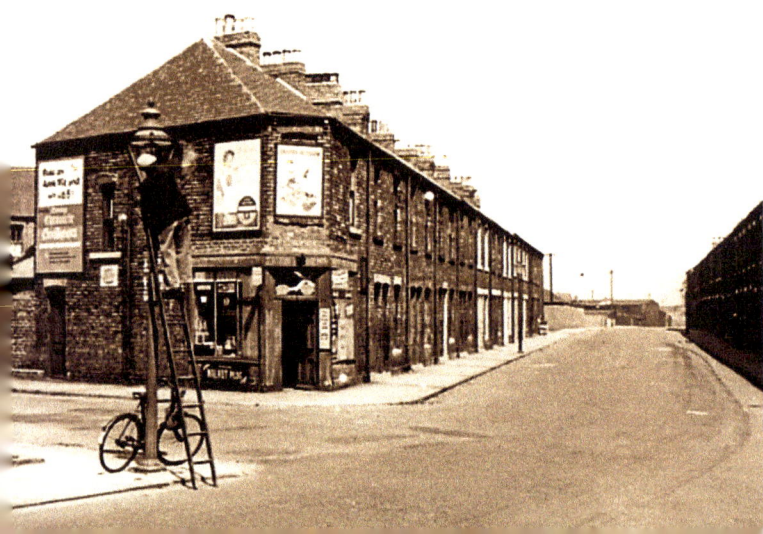

Lamplighter at the junction of Buddle Street and Commercial Road, 1952.

Little Ireland

It is well known locally that for many years Jarrow was known as Little Ireland. This evolved after an influx of Irish immigrant workers settled here, making Jarrow their home. One man in particular, born in Jarrow to a lovely Irish family, Thomas O'Connor was a very likeable character. He was well known in the town and a respected seafaring man, who in everyday conversation would lapse into seagoing jargon. For example, when referring to someone not very bright he would say 'he's as thick as that bulkhead' while pointing to a wall in the pub, or if you were attending a function to which Thomas had been invited and offered a lift, he would reply, 'no thanks I will get there under my own steam'. His all-time classic was delivered one Sunday afternoon at the Royal Oak Hotel when a friend of his was hospitalised to have a stomach operation. When asked by another of his friends how his pal was, Thomas replied. 'not very good, he's just had a complete midsection removed'.

Local Government

In the eighteenth century, there was no organised council to speak of. The unit of government was the Vestry, which consisted of twelve men who dealt with matters now handled by the local authority. The civil and ecclesiastical affairs and welfare of the people of the parish of St Paul came under the jurisdiction of a body known as the 'Twelve Gentlemen of the Vestry', who administered and made assessments for the 'Poor Law' by collecting money for the relief of needy inhabitants. Another of their tasks was for the upkeep of the fabric of St Paul's Church. They also appointed two highway surveyors whose responsibility it was to ensure that local roads and highways were kept in a reasonable state of repair, which was funded by a levy borne by those who used them. This organisation had very limited powers, but still managed to fulfil their duties until it was disbanded in 1850.

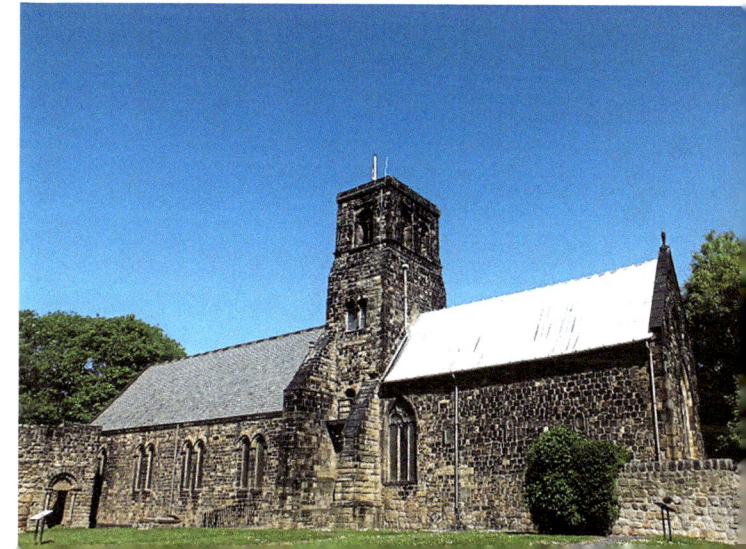

St Paul's Church, headquarters of the 'twelve men of the vestry' until 1850.

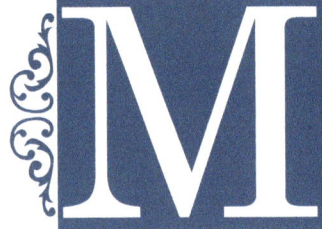

Monkton Stadium

Financing from the town's three major employers, Jarrow Metals, Tube Works and Palmers, led to the creation of the Metupa Sports Ground at Monkton. The venue and its facilities were used extensively for many years by the three company's programme of recreation and sporting events. Sadly, the stadium fell into a state of disrepair, but was rescued in 1936, funded and refurbished by 200 unemployed men under the Jarvis Scheme and co-operation of the town council. Upon completion in 1937, the venue became known as the Jarrow Cycling & Athletics Club, with Bob Charlton duly elected as club secretary. Further changes in the club's history took place in 1969, when it was renamed the Jarrow & Hebburn Athletics Club. After the passing of Bob Charlton in 1985, the late Jimmy Hedley became the driving force behind the club's activities, who found recognition in mentoring internationally known athletes Steve Cram and David Sharpe. South Tyneside Council recognised the importance of the stadium and the prestige it brought to the area, and invested in a comprehensive development programme during the 1980s, providing a new track and a 1,000-seat stand, together with a host of modern and up-to-date facilities. Now known in the area as Monkton Stadium, it is one of the region's major athletics venues, hosting both regional and national track and field events, providing coaching in many sports in its indoor and outdoor facilities.

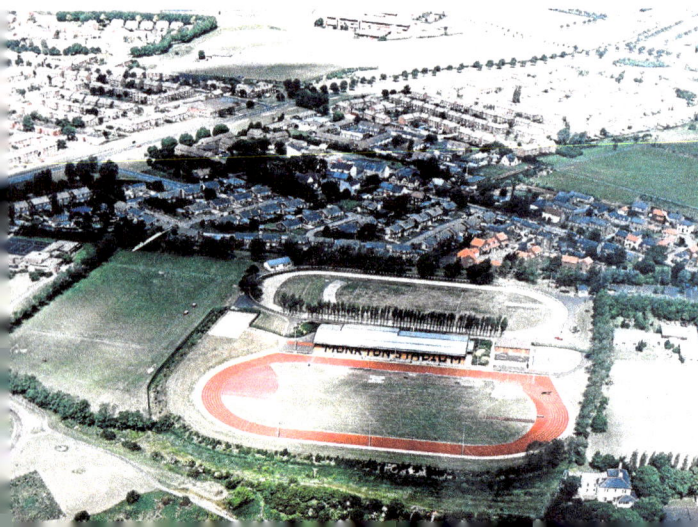

Monkton Stadium.

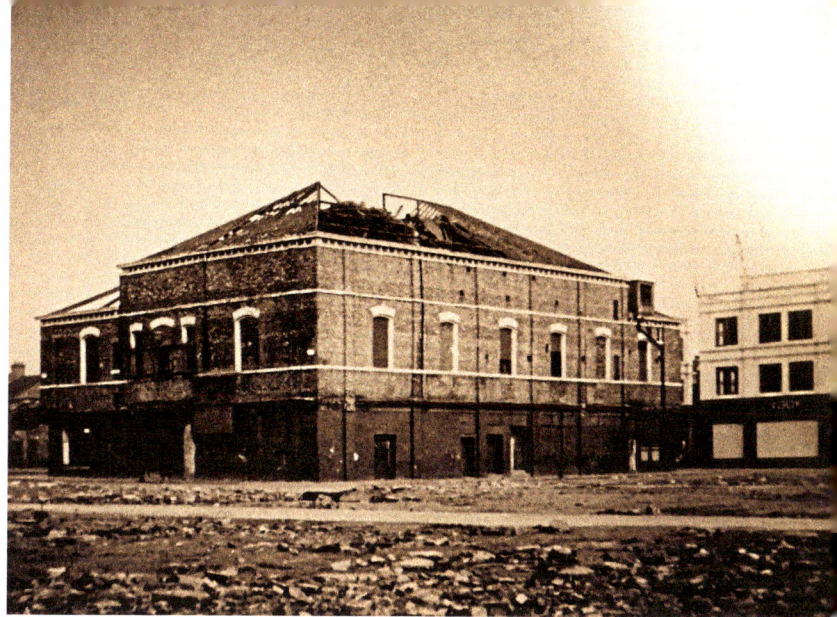

Theatre Royal,
Market Square,
1962.

Market Square

The Theatre Royal in the Market Square was built in 1866, and extensively refurbished in 1894, and again in 1898. From this time the theatre was partly used as a cinema screening films up until the beginning of the First World War, but was generally used for live theatre until around 1940. The building lay derelict until it was demolished in 1962, making way for a housing development. The town council who were responsible for the demolition of the building declined a quote of £16,000 for the work. Realising the quote was out of the question, they did accept a price of £600 from another source. The resulting rubble was removed and formed the base of the Lindisfarne roundabout at Primrose, which was under construction around the same time. Quite close to the Market Square was a private club The Excelsior, which later became Labour Party headquarters prior to them relocating to Park Road.

Modern Alternative Housing

Most of the food eaten during the 1940s and the early years of the 1950s would be unrecognisable to a twenty-first-century family. Although healthy and nutritious due to the absence of sugar and preservatives, most of it was unappealing and visually unappetising. Cooking became less of a chore as we entered a new and modern era. The invention of fast freezing during the '50s was perhaps the beginning of the changes to our eating habits. As the 1960s dawned, there was considerable improvement in the quality of life in Jarrow. People had a far superior lifestyle to what they were used to just a few years before. Houses with electric light and hot running water had suddenly become a reality, and were a vast improvement from the dilapidated Victorian houses with outside toilets, which were disappearing as fast as they were being vacated.

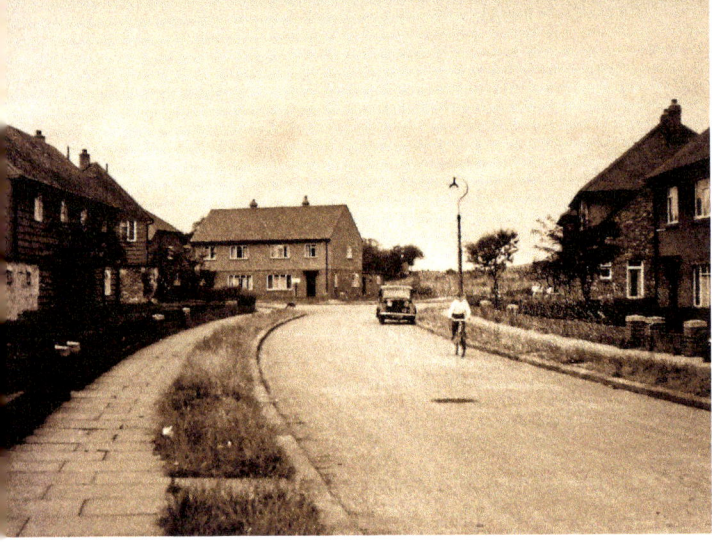

Modern alternative housing at Salcombe Avenue, 1955.

Mercantile Dry Dock & Engineering Co. Ltd

Due to the success of the Palmer Empire, Gavin Smith and his consortium of businessmen recognised the need for a shipyard specialising in ship repair close to the mouth of the River Tyne. A price was negotiated for a site on the south bank, and excavation work on a dry dock commenced in 1885. While many thousands of tons of earth were removed, wooden buildings were erected, which became the fitting, joiner and boiler shops. A paint shop and material stores department were also created in another part of the yard. Four years later, in 1889, offices were built, cranes erected and a workforce assembled. The Mercantile Dry Dock & Engineering Co. was in business,

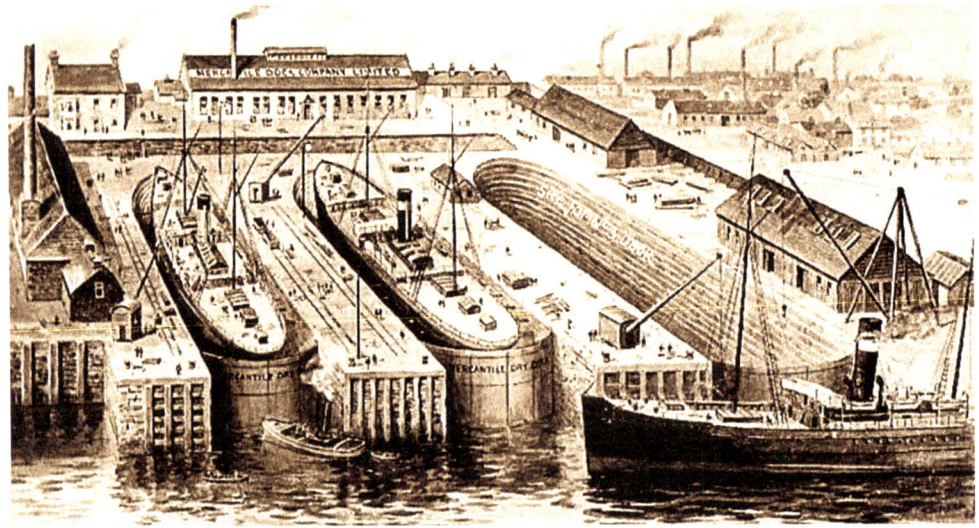

Engraving of Mercantile Dry Dock & Co. Ltd.

and was to repair many thousands of vessels (large and small) from the four corners of the earth for almost a century. As the order book swelled, so did the workforce, and by 1890 the need for a second dry dock became evident as queues of ships moored in the Tyne awaiting repair. Number two dock was opened on 4 August 1892. Eventually dry dock number three came along in 1908, and a fourth in 1960. This was completed to accommodate the larger vessels that were now beginning to make up the world's fleets. The company became a subsidiary of Northeast Coast Ship Repairers in 1966 and a constituent company of Court Line in 1977, formerly operating as part of the giant British Shipbuilders Ltd. The Tyne Ship Repair Group was to take over the yards operations until its demise in 1981.

Monkton Village

'Monkton is an ancient possession of Jarrow, with the *name* carrying its own derivation.' These words were penned by author and historian Robert Surtees in his *History and Antiquities of the County & Palatine of Durham* in 1816. Tradition assigns this ancient little village as the birthplace of the Venerable Bede. There is evidence of medieval construction from the sixth century at Bede Cottage, Grange Farm and a residence known as the Grange; there were a further two buildings of which little is known, but is believed that these five structures collectively formed the basis of the Monkton village we are familiar with today. After the death of Bede in 735, the Jarrow monastery suffered severely after being invaded on two separate occasions by Viking warriors, and left in ruins for centuries. By 1083 the monks that once inhabited the monastery were relocated to Chester le Street, but it is believed some of the monks remained in a cell at Monkton and another close by at Hebburn. There has been a

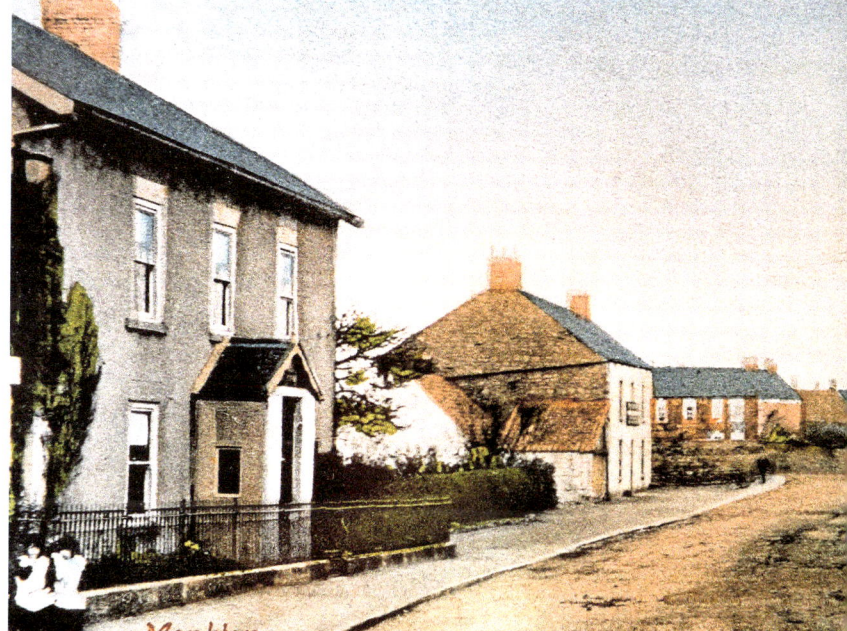

Monkton village, alleged birthplace of the Venerable Bede.

residence on the site of the Grange since 1539, and was most certainly a single-storey building. The owner Richard Marshall made considerable changes to this simple dwelling around 1662. This can be confirmed by an independent study of the church commissioner's renewal books held within the prior's kitchen at Durham Cathedral. In 1662, the value of the Grange was £50; three years later, in 1665, the value had risen considerably to £150. This re-evaluation was due to the addition of a second storey to the house. Further developments followed in the early part of the eighteenth century and the building, similar to what it is today, was completed in 1733. A clause in the deeds of the property state, 'the current owner whoever that may be, shall supply the village with water from its well at the time of drought.' This ancient clause is currently still in force.

Masonic Hall

Freemasonry is fraternal organisations that trace their origins to the local fraternities to the craft of stonemasons, which from the end of the fourteenth century regulated the qualifications of the craft of the stonemason, and their relationship with authorities and clients. The Masonic lodge is the basic organisational unit of Freemasonry. The lodge meets on a regular basis, similar to any small organisation, to conduct formal and routine business, which includes the organisation of social and charitable events, and to discuss the prospect of new members. As the formalities conclude, the lodge usually adjourn for a dinner, which is preceded with speeches and toasting. The foundation stone for the Masonic hall in Grange Road was laid on 21 April 1881 by Brother George Spain. The proceedings commenced with an emergency lodge held in the Mechanics Institute in Ellison Street. The brothers marched in procession in full Masonic regalia via Ormonde Street, Market Square and Grange Road to the site of the stone-laying ceremony. The procession was led by the band of the Durham Voluntary

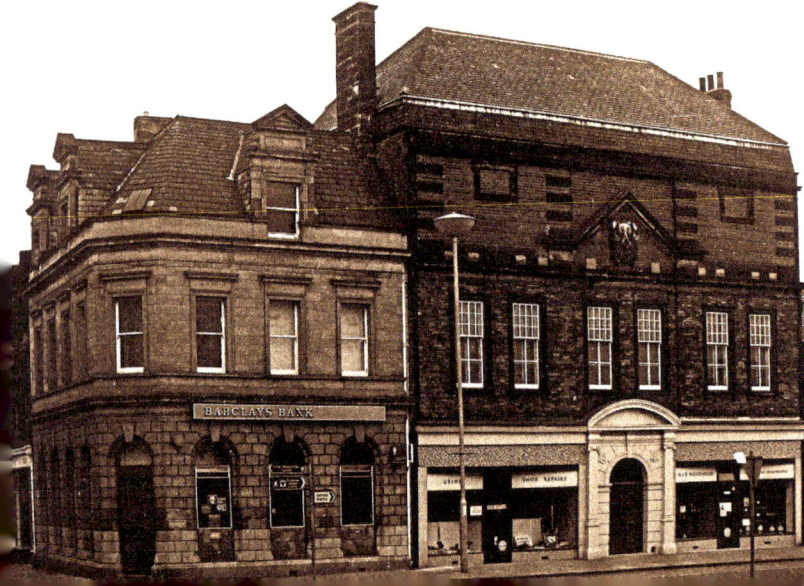

Masonic hall (to the right of this image) in Grange Road.

Engineers and witnessed by hundreds of spectators. The hall was completed and ready for the grand opening ceremony in February 1882.

Mayfield Girls' School

As the trend for building schools continued, extensions to the existing buildings became evident as the population continued to rise. Monkton Road School in 1880 was now accommodating the infants, juniors and seniors under one roof. The clergy and church committee were considering the possibility of the construction of another school to relieve the overcrowded situation at Monkton Road. The problem was resolved with a school at Grant Street in 1885. In 1925, the parish purchased two large houses in Pine Street with the intention of creating another school. A costly conversion of the two properties resulted in the creation of Mayfield Senior Girls' School. Pupils were transferred from Grant Street upon completion and the school opened in 1928. Grant Street remained as an infant school until it suffered a direct hit by an enemy bomb in a night attack in 1941. The building was devastated and subsequently demolished soon after, and as a consequence the children were moved to and educated at Mayfield.

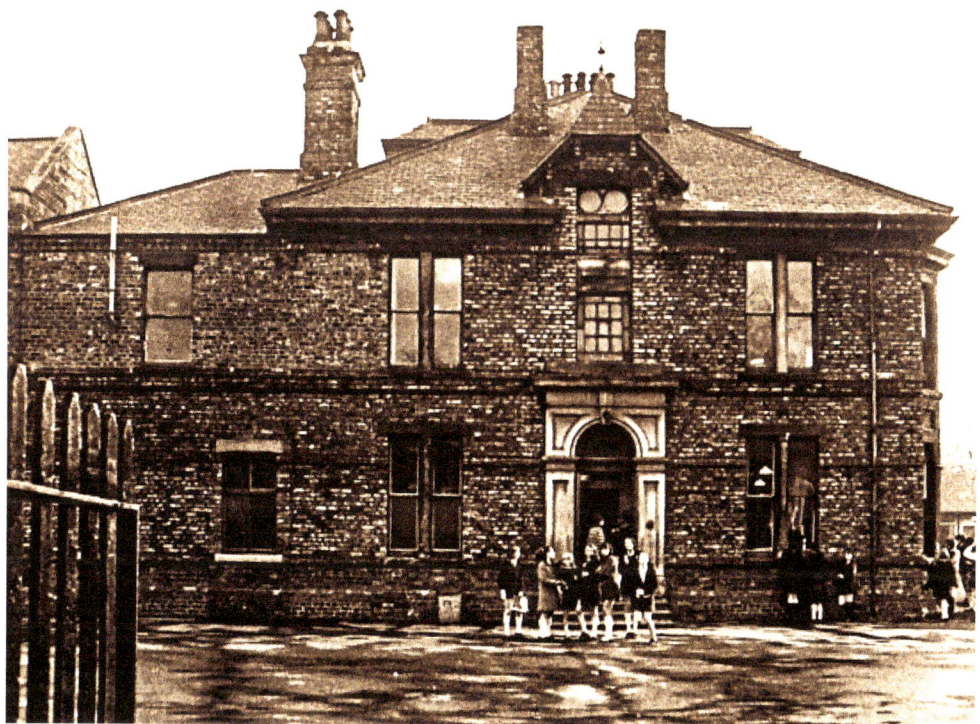

Mayfield Girls' School.

North Eastern Hotel

A request from shipyard boss Charles Palmer for accommodation in the form of a hotel for the many world dignitaries and VIPs who travelled to the town bringing trade with them, and for the many medical staff from the Palmer Memorial Hospital close by, prompted the construction of the fifteen-bedroom North Eastern Hotel and restaurant. Having served its purpose as a hotel up until the 1940s, and no longer enjoying Palmers' custom, the hotel ceased trading as a residential establishment and was purchased by Newcastle Breweries Ltd. The premises traded as a public house and restaurant up until 1994 and was demolished in 1995. The area the mighty building once covered now serves the town as a car park for a supermarket chain.

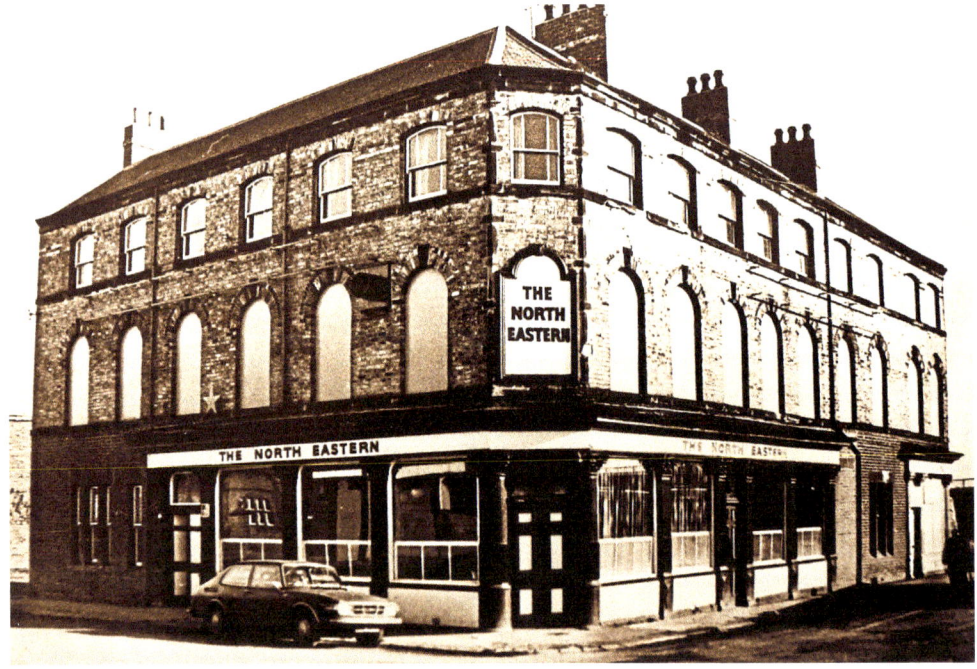

North Eastern Hotel.

Northern Bus Station

Jarrow has had a reliable and efficient transport system since the inauguration of the tram service in 1906. From 1929 when the service was discontinued at the introduction of the motor bus, although still primitive and most uncomfortable passengers, passengers were able to travel much further, with regular services to South Shields, Newcastle and beyond. Charlton's solid rubber-clad wheeled buses, easily recognisable in blue and white livery, wound their way through the streets of Jarrow, often with their engines overheating, for many years. As the population of the town grew so did the need for a more modern and up-to-date service. This was entrusted to Northern General Transport Co., who had previously introduced a modern fleet of vehicles in depot at South Shields, and were eager to branch out into Jarrow. Prior to the construction of the projected depot and garages at Station Street in the town centre in 1954, a series of bus stops were conveniently located at intervals along Ellison Street. By the 1990s a depot of these dimensions was deemed uneconomical, as more and more commuters were now using the Tyne & Wear Metro. As a consequence, the old depot was demolished and replaced with a much smaller and streamlined bus terminal.

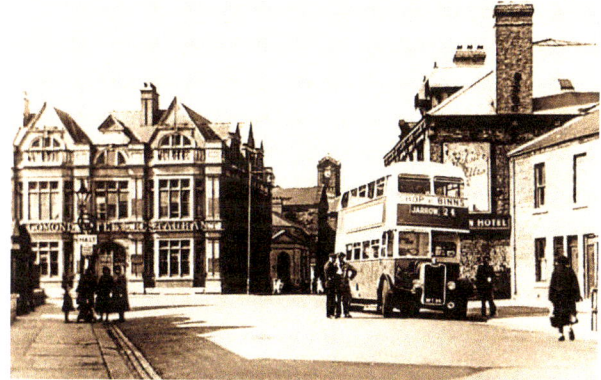

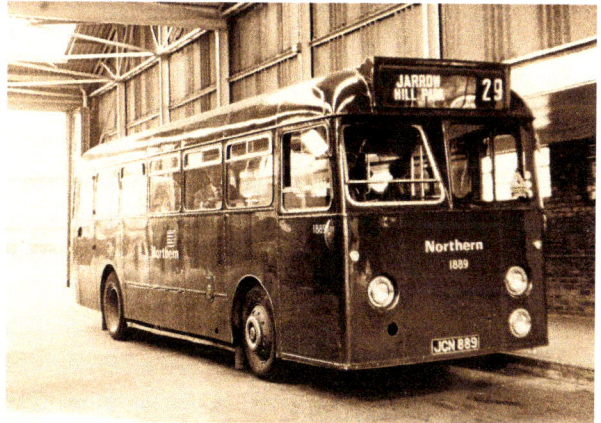

Northern Bus Depot prior to 1954, and bus sheds in 1966.

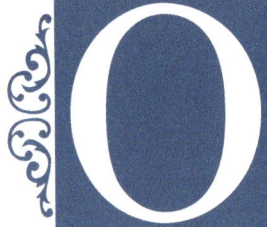

Outdoor Pursuits

During the long hot summer months of the 1950s, we turned into a nation of picnickers who delighted in eating outdoors as personal disposable income improved, and the need for quality time with family became important. People worked hard in those days, and believed they had earned at least one day a week away from it all. The simple British pastime of driving off for the day for a picnic in a meadow by a clear lazily flowing stream with a basket of sandwiches and a Victoria sponge was appealing to those who were lucky enough to have transport. Perhaps this pleasure of eating al fresco was inherited from our continental cousins, to whom it was quite common and an accepted way of life. For Jarrow folk without transport, venues such as Harrison's Field, Charlie's Park or the beaches at South Shields were all that was required for a carefree day out with the family.

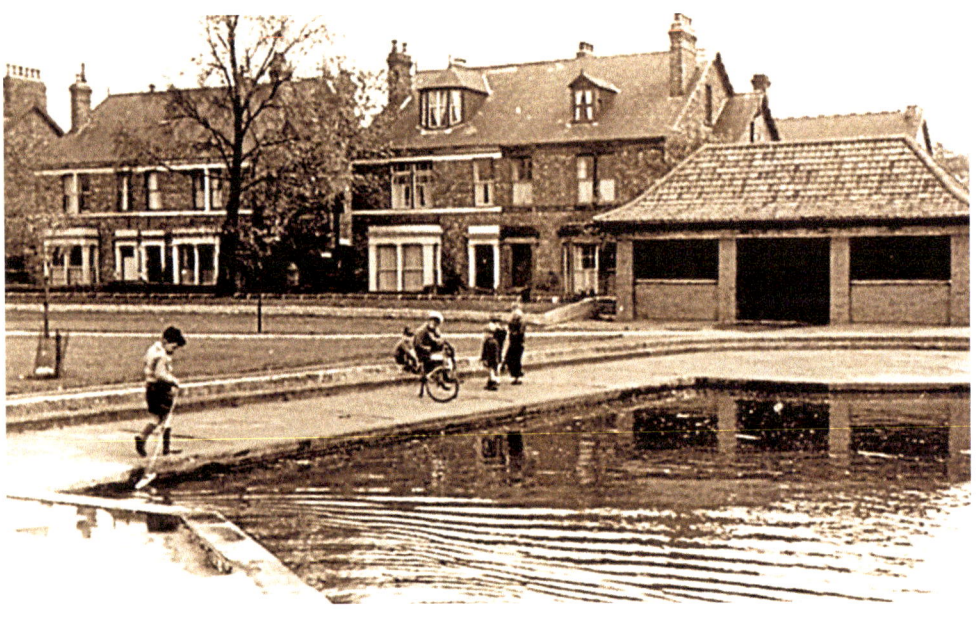

West Park, 1955.

Ode to a Crusade

The Palmers' Shipyard was closed down, Jarrow was in decline.
No more the riveter's hammer was heard upon the Tyne
And as the dole queue lengthened, frustrated men were many,
a job they all were wanting to earn an honest penny.

Despite the many meetings, the worries and the fears
Jarrow's plea to government fell upon deaf ears
After many months of planning, it was then decided
'We'll take a petition to London' we won't be derided.

In nineteen hundred and thirty six, two hundred men good and true
set out to walk to London town; there was nothing else to do
As they left the town hall and marched up Grange Road West,
the send off for the heroes, was nothing but the best.

The sun it shone so brightly as they walked the first twelve miles,
the banter and the old jokes the laughter and the smiles.
At last they could all rest and soak their aching feet,
the first leg had been completed; they had reached Chester le Street.

Soon the march reached Yorkshire; they were given such a cheer.
A bath, a meal, a change of clothes and a couple of pints of beer
Some of the marchers rested, others went to a show
Others read their mail from home 'Oh how we miss you so.

Wee Ellen and Davy Riley walking proudly did not yield
Leading the 'so proud' marchers as they entered Chesterfield
The mouth organ played the old tunes, the singing was the best
The Jarrow lads were happy as they travelled on their quest

The cobblers of Leicester played their part 'that's right'
Repairing the old boots, they toiled all through the night.
The people of the Midlands, did their best no doubt
The crusaders were uplifted, 'three cheers' they did shout.

At last London came into view, the rain it pelted down
There wasn't a cordial welcome for the lads of Jarrow town
Led by wee Ellen, they'd walked through rain and sun
But a last, they all could say. 'right lads good job done'

Con Shields and Albert Sewell, Con Whalen and there's more
John Kelly and Bill Beattie are famous names of yore
Joe Bradley and Dave Mc Kenna, a fine young Scottish laddie
Two hundred heroes one and all, with a dog called Paddy.

So many years have gone by since that famous March
When Jarrow's bold crusaders walked up Marble Arch
With their patched up boots and shoes, and old shirts made of cotton
Those famous men from Jarrow will never be forgotten.

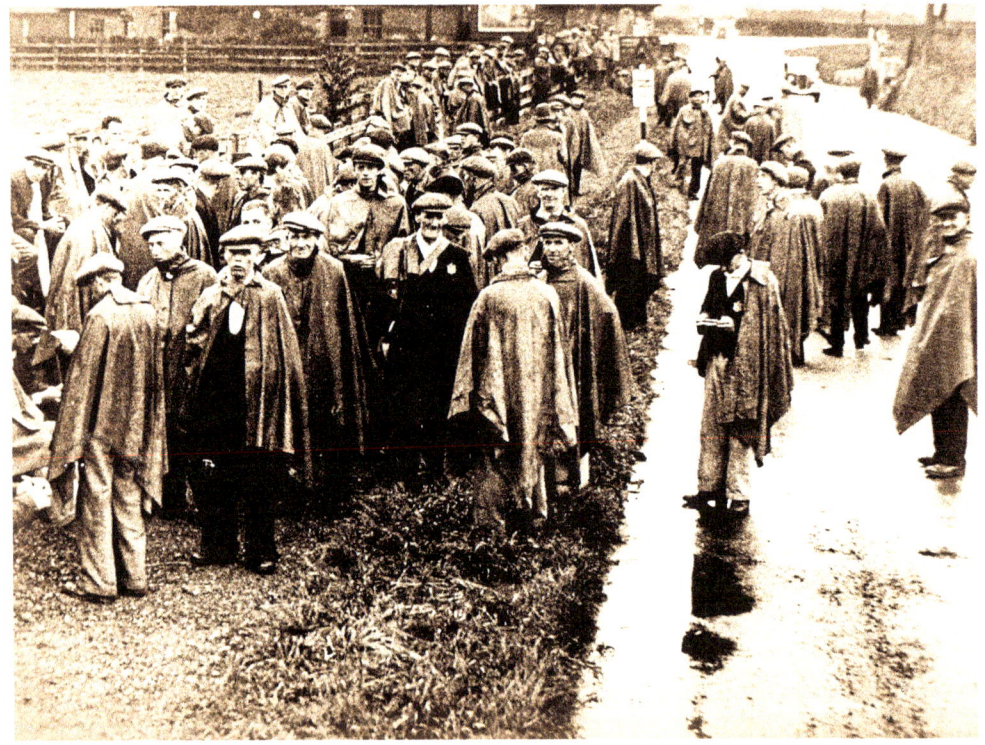

The rain-soaked 'Crusaders' stop for lunch in North Yorkshire.

P

Paper Mill

Paper manufacture in Jarrow commenced in 1841 and continued until 1860 when the mill Thomas Bell operated was taken over by successful businessman and Quaker William Henry Richardson, who after employing scores of men, women and children at the paper mill at Springwell, channelled his energies into worthwhile activities for the good of the town, particularly in the cause of education. The mill at Springwell was constantly under the threat of fire due to the enormous quantities of esparto grass stored there. The grass was one of the prime constituents in paper manufacture at that time. Another great fire witnessed in 1898 was a blaze at Grange Farm, Monkton, when twelve or more haystacks caught fire, along with several outbuildings, which as a result were completely destroyed. Fire tenders from Palmers, Gateshead and

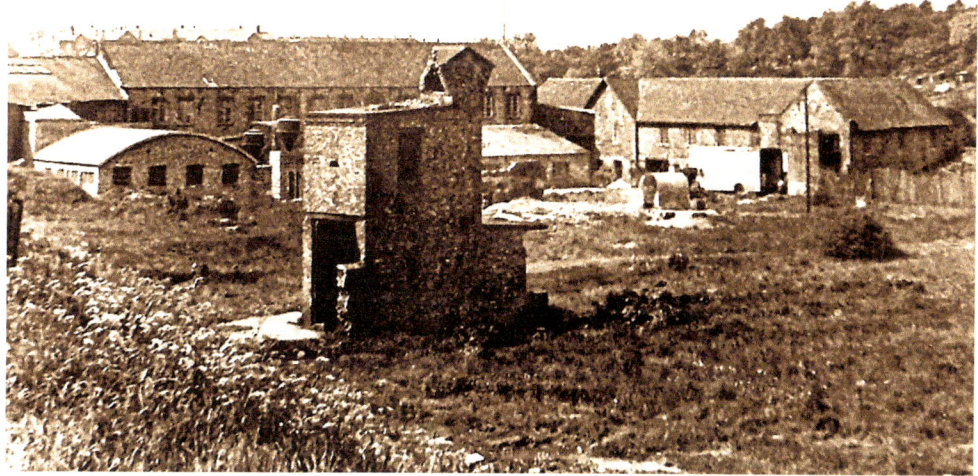

Former paper mill at Springwell.

Jarrow attended the scene, but the inefficient water supply prevented the firefighters from bringing the blazing haystacks and buildings under control. The frequency and severity of localised fires, especially within the farming community, prompted a meeting of the Monkton Parish Council with a view to purchase firefighting equipment. The manual appliance was to serve the community and assist where necessary. Tenders were submitted, with one for £72 being accepted. The breakdown reads: £53 for the engine, the hose and reel for £15, and engine shafts with accessories priced at £4.

Public Houses

Scores of narrow terraced streets networked the town centre from the middle of the Victorian era, many of which had a public house nestled between the tiny terraced houses, with others towards the end of the terraces. These hostelries remind us that the community lived side by side for decades in the shadow of industry. At the annual general meeting of the town's licensing committee of 1896, it was revealed the town had twenty-eight public houses, twenty-three beerhouses and two off-licensed premises, totalling fifty-three in all. The presiding committee took any misbehaviour seriously and reported that in the past year six landlords were charged with allowing drunkenness, with four being dismissed from holding a license in the foreseeable future. Of a town with a population of 36,000, 500 cases of being drunk and disorderly were heard by local magistrates.

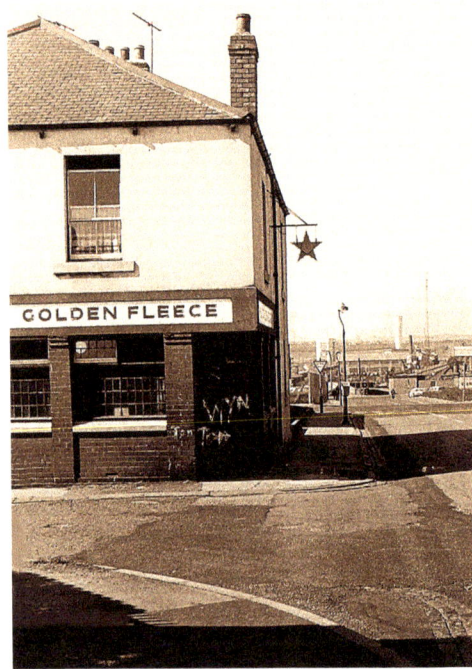

Golden Fleece, Ferry Street, one of the town's fifty-four public houses.

Palmers' Shipyard

Charles Mark Palmer, together with his brother George, were to bring work and prosperity to the town in 1851. The brothers commenced the business of shipbuilding under the name of Palmer Bros & Co. The days of wooden ships had not passed but the company recognised that this was coming to an end. Their first major project *John Bowes* was launched in 1852; this vessel was the world's first collier with a revolutionary iron screw. In subsequent years the 140-acre shipyard housed eight miles of internal railway, and boasted a 10,000-strong workforce. Palmers' was more than a shipyard, and rose to be one of the country's first integrated businesses. Its operations covered the transportation of iron ore aboard its own fleet of vessels from the company's mines at Port Mulgrave in Yorkshire. The thousands of tons of coal required to fuel the furnaces came from the company's own mines, again in Yorkshire. The success story was aided with the use of a unique steel-rolling process and an impressive galvanising plant reputed to be the busiest and most up to date in the whole of the British Isles. The population boom – from 3,000 in 1851 to a staggering 33,000 in 1893 – was evidence of the grip Palmers held on the town. With this influx of people, the town prospered beyond all expectations as the company was capable of producing high-grade merchant and naval vessels. In 1907, there was a terrific slump in the shipbuilding industry. By 1910 slow progress had been made but recovery was not going to happen overnight. The fractures were concealed by the outbreak of the First World War. Eventually this war was to be the solution Palmers was desperately seeking, replacing the war losses with bigger and better ships in 1920. By 1927 the yard was back on track and in full production supplying

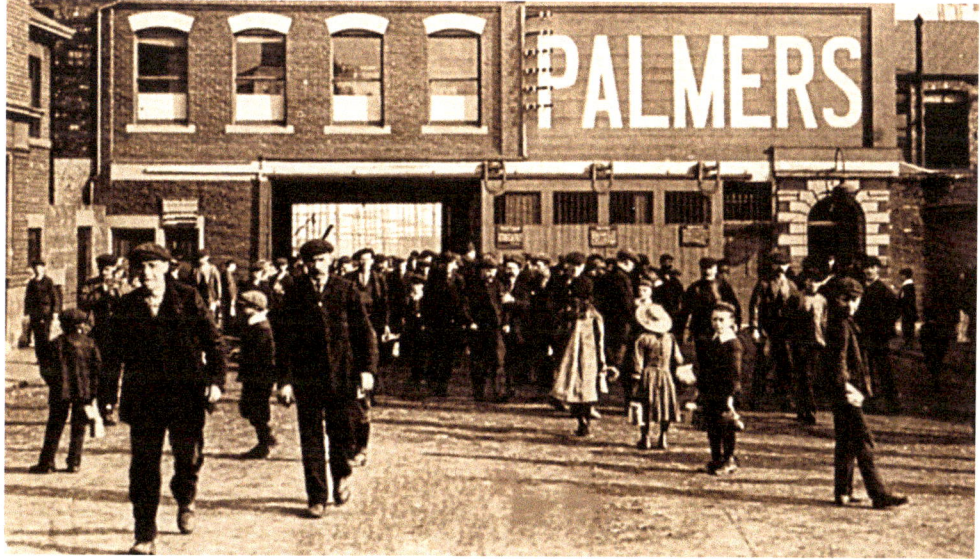

Palmers gates, 1912.

the urgently required warships and merchant vessels. As the 1930s dawned, the now fragile and fractured infrastructure of the company became evident as the depression tightened its powerful grip. Palmers was unable to ride out the current economical storm. The last ship to sail from the yard was HMS *Duchess* in 1932. No fewer than 1,007 ships were launched at the yard, equivalent to 2,000,000 tonnes, but this world-famous shipyard was to grind to a standstill within a few short years. By 1934 it was all over: Palmers was no more. The company went into receivership with the massive workforce sadly joining the ever lengthening dole queue as unemployment in Jarrow was accelerating towards 88 per cent.

Parkland

Jarrow was a crowded town during the 1930s, as most of the migrants who arrived at the beginning of the century when the town flourished decided it was here they wanted to remain and rear their families. A high percentage of these settlers were of Irish decent, and Jarrow assumed the title 'Little Ireland' as it was known for a number of years after their arrival. Acres of green belted land were donated and set aside solely for recreation purposes, the first; West Park was given by wealthy landowners Sir Walter and Lady James in 1876. The creation of the Drewett Playing Fields came about in 1912. A temperance ground at Primrose was converted to Springwell Park, rose beds were created along with sunken flower gardens. The Longmore Memorial Fountain, which stood for many years in the town centre, was relocated to a prime site in the

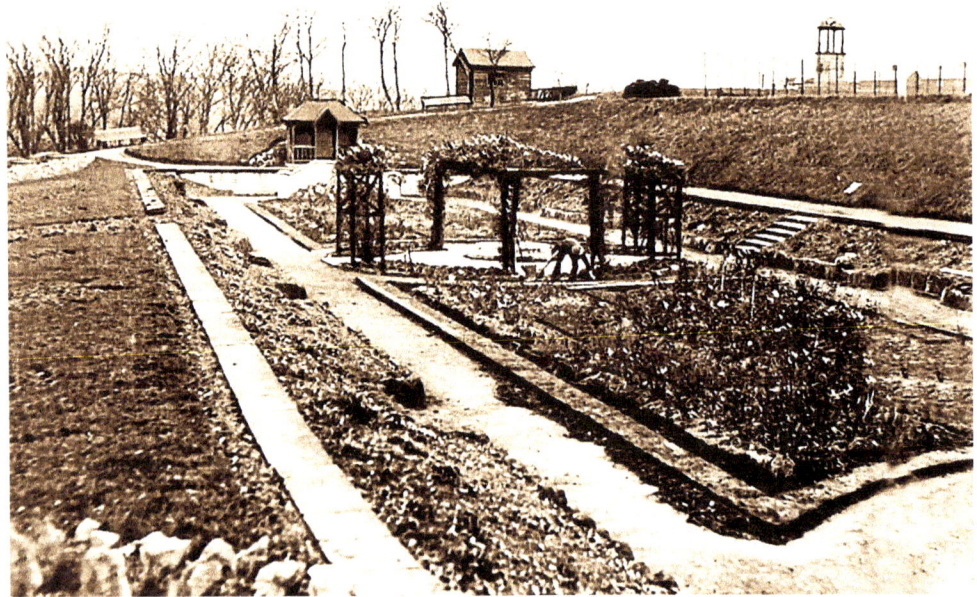

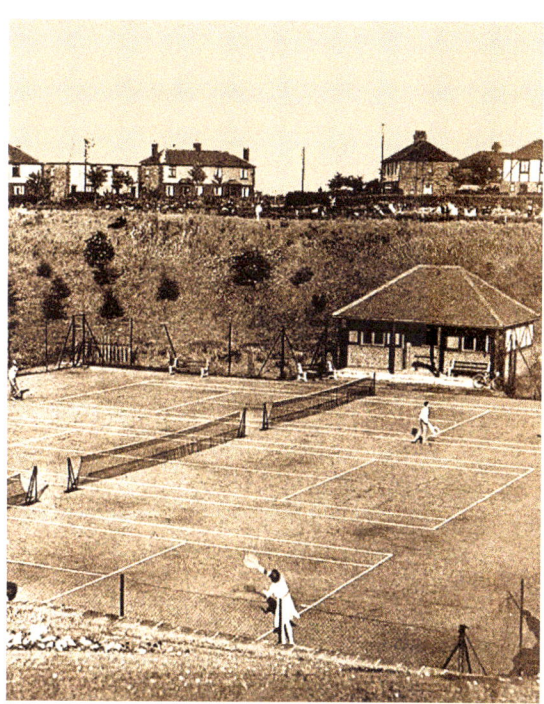

Opposite and right: Springwell Park rose beds and tennis courts, Jarvis Park.

park in 1921. Jarvis Park is more familiarly known as Valley View Park, and close by is Monkton Dene Park. Of the towns five parklands, Springwell and Monkton Dene were designed without amenities, just quiet and pleasant peaceful places to be. Paddling pools, tennis courts and bowling greens were among the attractions of the others.

Pub Crawl

Where are the pubs of yesteryear which filled us with great cheer
We threw our darts and sang the songs and supped that lovely beer
Where are the pubs of Jarrow town, nice thoughts still remain
So just sit back, enjoy the crack, and walk down memory lane

The Borough, The Globe and Harbour Lights, The Cottage with its charms
The Albion, Grange and Staith House. Not forgetting The Forrester's Arms
The Hylton Castle painted green, The Alkali painted red
The Royal Oak, The Prince of Wales, and of course the old Queens Head

The Western and The Rolling Mill together side by side
And the beer in the East Ferry Inn, was affected by the tide
Along the road the old Bridge Inn, stood there on its own
And the beer in the Telegraph made the old men groan

The Allison Arms, the Alexander, the Golden Lion too
Rose & Crown, the Alnwick Castle all sold the blue star brew
The Queens Arms, and the Queens Hotel packed them in all standing
The Commercial pub 'oh what a view, is that the ferry landing

Who will forget the Forge & Hammer with its caged monkey so cute
The County and Duke of Wellington known as the 'boot'
The Crown & Anchor in 42' quenched the wartime fears
As did the Tynemouth Castle, North Eastern and the Engineers

The Ben Lomond, what a crowd 'right lads form a queue'
The Golden Fleece, a fine old name of which there numbered two
The Lord Nelson in Walter Street, in Hedworth Lane the Greyhound
The Royal bar in Market Square, sold ten pints for a pound

The Lord Nelson in Monkton village, was once among the farms
The Station Hotel, managed by Fred, further down the Ellison Arms
And what about the old Bell Rock, a real blast from the past
Finally, the Robin Hood we save the best til' last

I hope you enjoyed your little walk and memories are clear
Of happy nights, and sometimes fights of days no longer here
Though things change and time moves on, and good friends drift apart
Those memories of Jarrow pubs live forever in your heart.

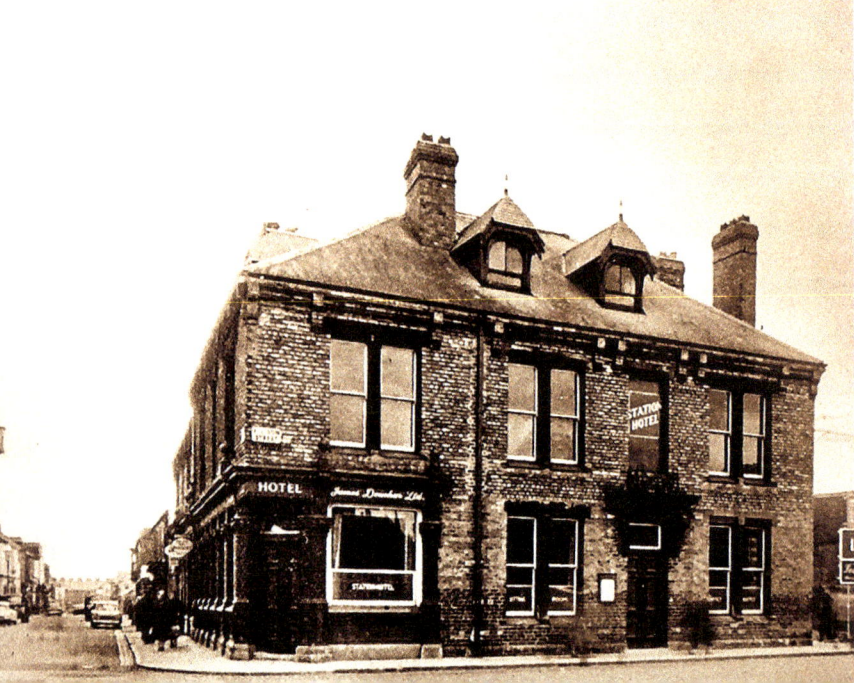

Globe Hotel,
Buddle Street.

Q

Queen Elizabeth II

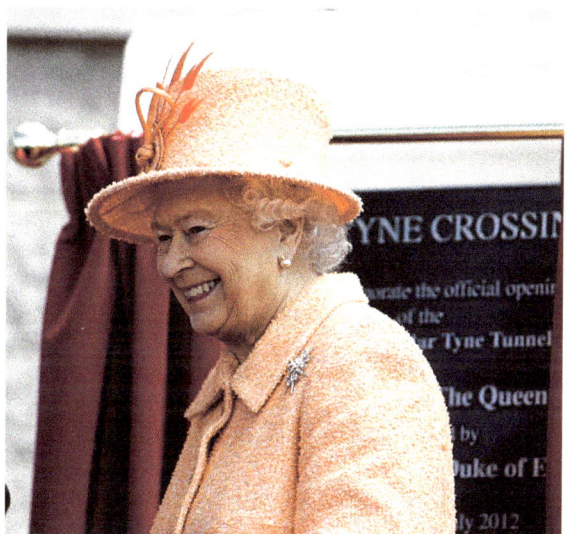

Her Majesty Queen Elizabeth at the opening of the Tyne Tunnel, 2012.

The region was honoured once again with a visit from two royal guests in 2012, Her Majesty Queen Elizabeth and her husband Prince Philip Duke of Edinburgh, who were invited to the auspicious occasion of officially opening the most recent Tyne crossing. The second road tunnel, which took four years to complete and cost £260 million, is designed to work in conjunction with the original tunnel from 1967.

Queen Elizabeth The Queen Mother

The Duke and Duchess of York visited Jarrow on the occasion of launching a battle cruiser for the Admiralty – HMS *York* – in 1928 from the Palmers' Shipyard in the town. On the same day, the royal couple officially opened York Avenue, which was allegedly the country's first dual carriageway.

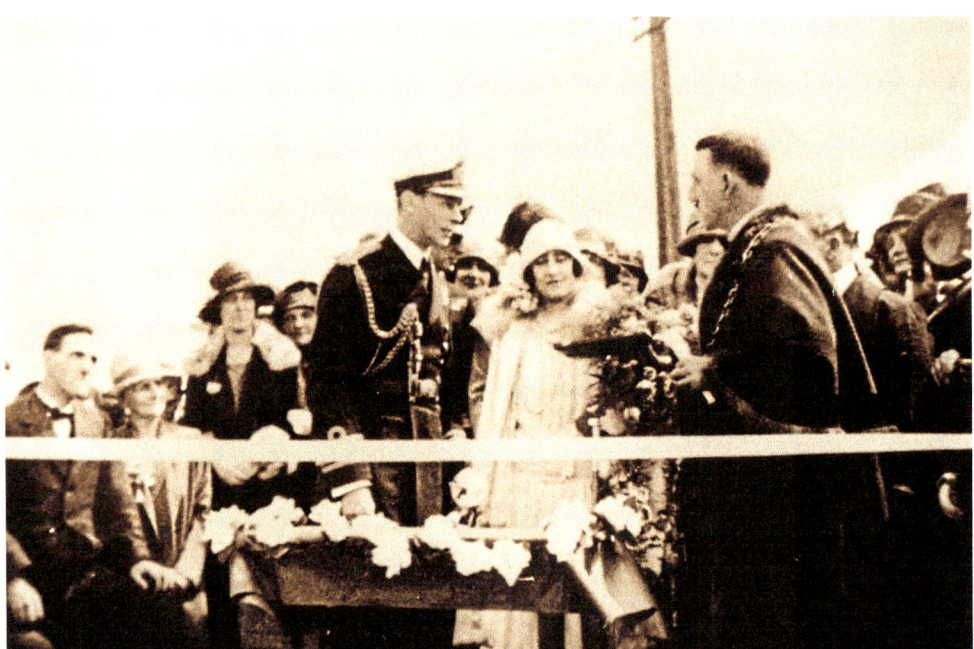

Her Majesty Queen Elizabeth The Queen Mother at Jarrow, 1928.

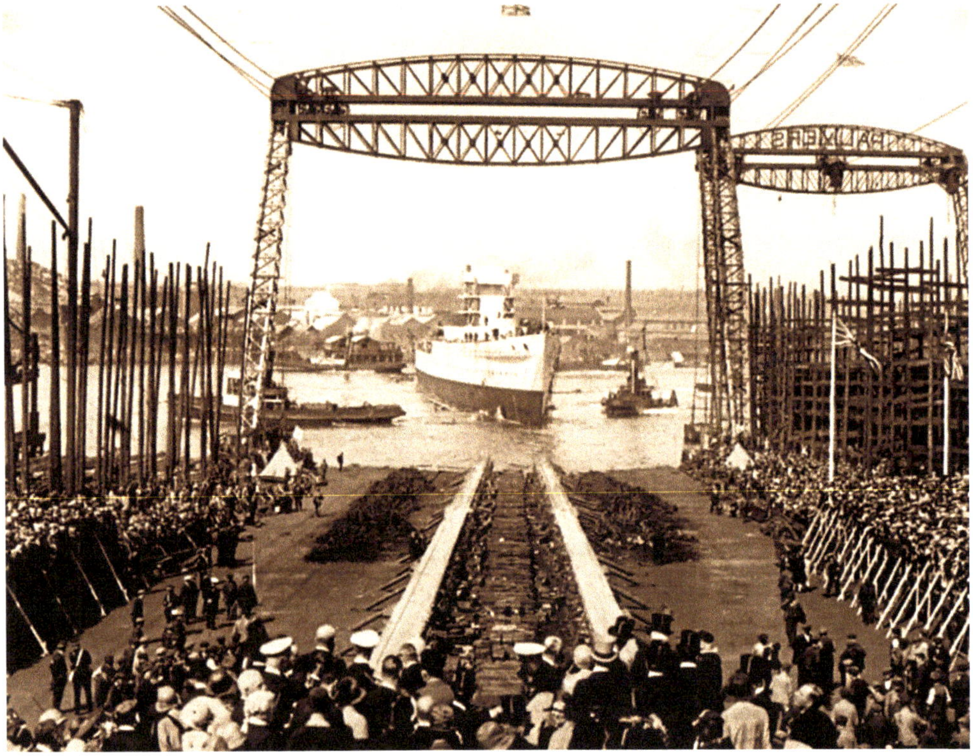

R

RMS *Berengaria*

Formerly called *Imperator* and built for the Hamburg–America line, RMS *Berengaria* was launched in May 1912, and at 52,000 tons was the world's largest vessel. The ship made her maiden voyage to New York in June 1913. The vessel was mothballed and anchored at Hamburg for protection from August 1914, and for the duration of the

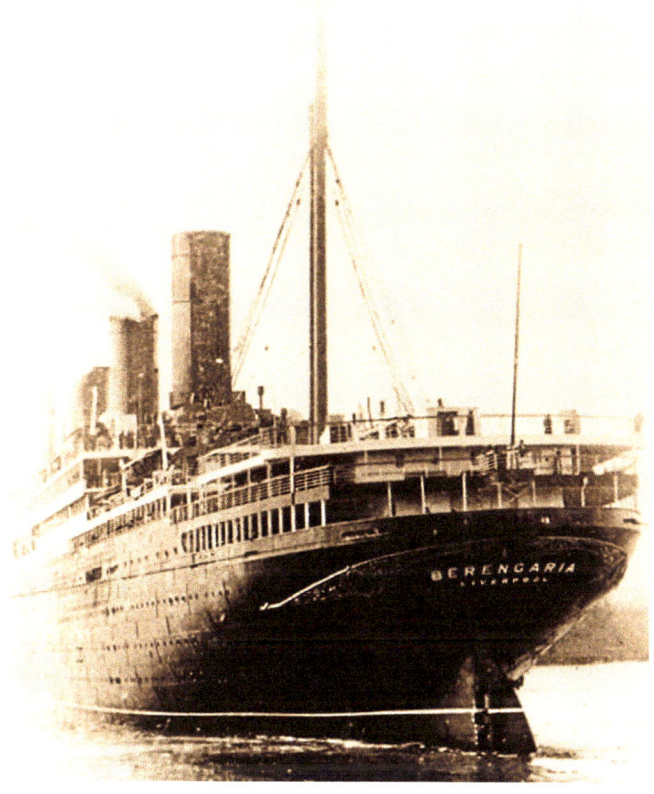

RMS *Berengaria* arriving at Jarrow, 1938.

First World War. In 1920, she was purchased by the Cunard Line, who, after becoming the company's flagship and pride of the fleet, changed her name to *Berengaria*. In 1934, Cunard merged with the White Star Line, but downgraded *Berengaria* at the arrival of the company's latest acquisition – the *Queen Mary* – in 1936. After a devastating fire, caused by defective wiring, on board the *Berengaria* in New York harbour, the vessel was withdrawn from service. After decommissioning, Sir John Jarvis purchased the ship in 1938 as scrap for £108,000, which was to be broken up at Jarrow, creating work for over 200 unemployed men. Their task was to remove the superstructure as far as the main deck level from the former luxurious liner. Visitors came from far and wide to get a glimpse of the elaborate fixtures and fittings from the giant vessel, and generated a further income after their auction, which was to top up the Surrey Fund. The German company responsible for the construction of the ship held the secret of producing concrete as hard as steel, which was used to secure the propeller shaft to the ship's hull. Several attempts were made to blast the concrete, all without success. Eventually fractures appeared in the hull of the ship, which had to be repaired prior to it being towed to a breakers yard in Scotland to complete the task. The resulting scrap metal was sold back to Germany, assisting their own financial crisis. They offered a steel tube rolling mill for the town in return for the sought after scrap metal. Sir John and the Corporation welcomed this gesture, recognising it as a further lease of life for the town and the prospect of work for its many unemployed. A new industry, the Tube Works, was born in 1938.

SS *John Bowes*

Built by Palmers in 1852 and launched in June of the same year, SS *John Bowes* was the world's first successful steam powered, water-ballasted collier with an iron screw propeller. Although she was rigged as a three-mast schooner as an additional means of power, the vessel was capable of carrying up to thirty keels of coal from the Tyne to London in a remarkable forty-eight hours, and discharging her 630-ton cargo in a further eighteen hours, and returning to the Tyne within a short space of time. This she achieved on her maiden voyage on 29 July 1852, completing the trip in five days – returning on August 3. The vessel's performance was carefully monitored as it was capable of doing the work in five days, compared to that which three similar-sized vessels could achieve in one month. Delighted with the vessel's performance, Palmers built a bigger vessel later that year – SS *James Dixon* – in a similar style to the *John Bowes*. *John Bowes* eventually ran aground off the northern coast of Spain in 1934 under the name of *Valentin Fierro*, after a remarkable long life of eighty-two years as a seagoing vessel.

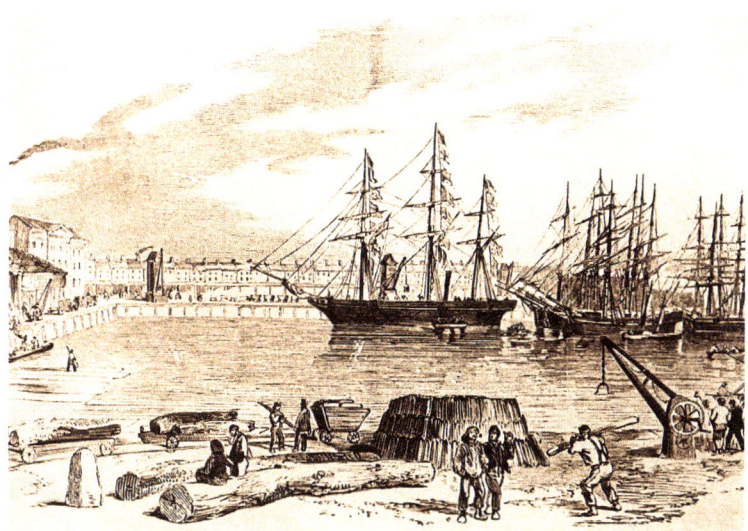

Iron screw collier SS *John Bowes* arriving at East India Docks, London, in 1852.

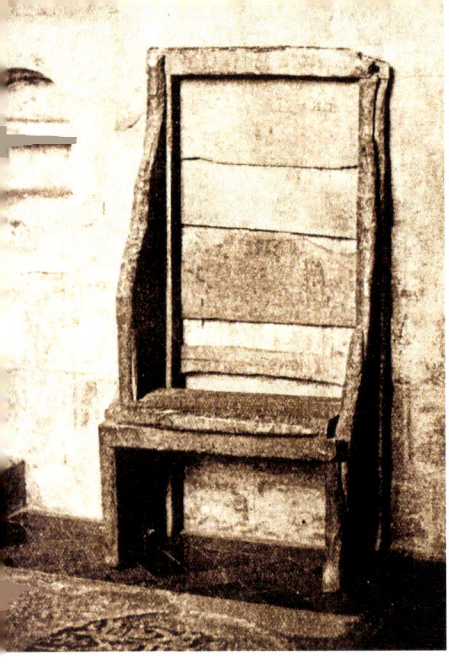

Bede's chair, St Paul's Church.

St Paul's Church

The chancel of St Paul's Church was founded in the year AD 681 prior to the arrival of Bede. The basilica wasn't built until later in the decade, and for many years there were two separate structures until the construction of the tower in 685, the same year the church was dedicated to St Paul, when the chancel, basilica and tower were recognised as one building. The present nave of the church was built over 1,000 years later in 1866, at the same time the north aisle was constructed, completing the church as we know it today. It is believed the resident monks hid themselves in the tower from the marauding Danes. A dedication stone recording this historic milestone is situated above the chancel arch. The translation reads, 'dedication of the church of St Paul on the ninth of the kalends of May in the fifteenth year of King Ecgfrith and the fourth year of Coelfrith, Abbott and with God's help the founder of this church'. Within the church sits, rather awkwardly, a crudely built little wooden chair. For centuries it was believed the chair possessed magical powers, and anyone sitting on it would be miraculously cured of any illness they may have. There was also a strong belief the chair was a cure for infertility, providing the infertile person removed a splinter of wood. Bede's chair, as it has always been known, is nothing more than legend, passed down from generation to generation, as Bede's bottom never actually graced the ancient little relic – carbon dating revealed it was made in the eleventh century.

Swimming Baths

Prior to the opening of the swimming baths in Walter Street by the Lady Mayoress Mrs C. M. James in 1911, the town had been provided with bathing facilities in a disused

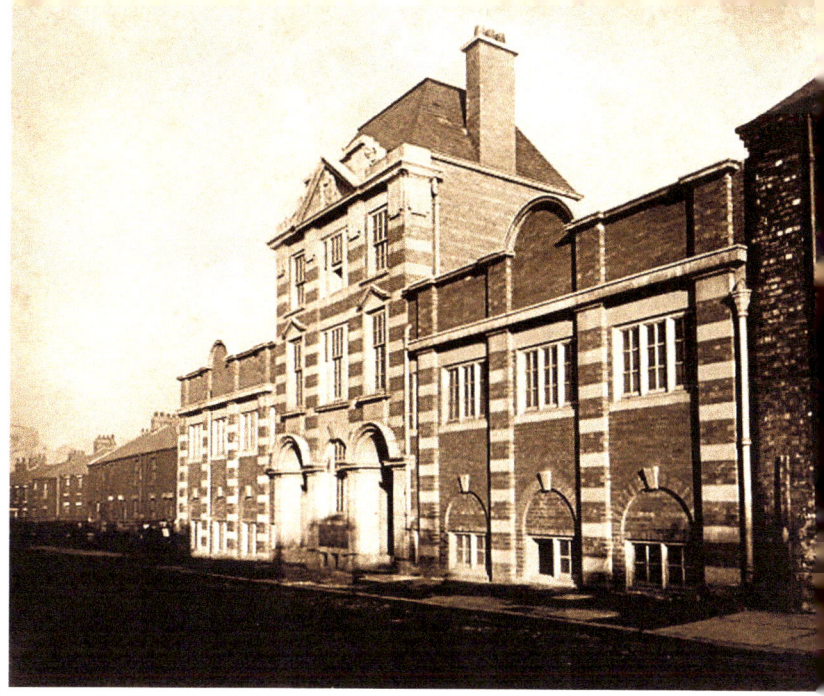

Swimming baths,
Walter Street, 1925.

furniture warehouse in Grange Road. The population of Jarrow were provided with the modern recreational facility of a swimming pool, which when covered doubled as a dance venue and physical training centre during the 1930s and '40s. By 1982 the tired old building had served its purpose and beyond refurbishment, as extensive facilities had been made available earlier at Temple Park Leisure Centre at South Shields and neighbouring Hebburn. Although the main attraction at the Walter Street complex was the full-size swimming pool, another was the 'public baths' as very few of the row upon row of Victorian houses in Jarrow had the luxury of a bath. As sanitation became a council priority, conditions rapidly improved with more and more houses being built with amenities. The need for the public baths decreased sufficiently for the service to be discontinued by the 1950s. Minor alterations were made to the ageing building in 1970, which included the installation of a sauna bath and solarium, prior to its demolition in 1984. The Hebburn complex was demolished, and Temple Park became obsolete when a single facility was provided and made available on the seafront at South Shields.

Ship Breaking

Jarrow has the natural advantage of being situated close to the deep waters of the River Tyne and has always been connected by good roads and rail communications to all centres of commerce. For many years Jarrow people relied on Palmers for their bread and butter, but sadly Palmers has gone, never to return. The vast area it once covered lay derelict, looming large and lifelike – a ghost from times gone by, waiting as if to haunt the present. Shipbuilding was not permitted here for forty years under a clause in the contract of sale of the new owners Shipbuilding Securities Co. Ltd.

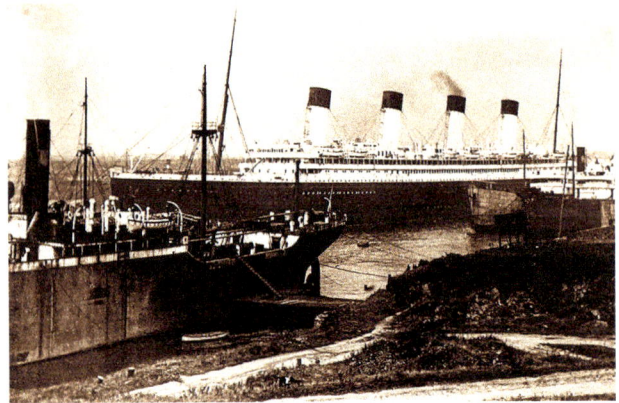

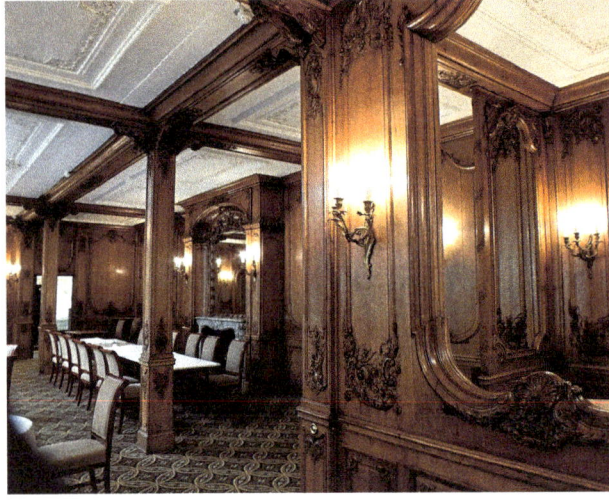

RMS *Olympic* arriving at Jarrow in 1938, and part of the magnificent wood panelling that graced her, which is now on display at The White Swan Hotel, Alnwick, Northumberland.

Nevertheless, it was to this barren land that the mighty John Jarvis was to look for any signs of renewed activity. 'If we can't build them, let's break them' he announced, and with these words a new industry was conceived. Though still in its embryonic stages, ship breaking commenced with the purchase of a Greek vessel by the Surrey Fund, which was sold to a firm of breakers on the most attractive terms to encourage them to test the viability of profitable work on our waters. The loss to the fund on this particular occasion was close to £1,000, a loss it could ill afford, but once again the northern territories rallied and covered the deficit. Apart from this minor setback, the experiment was deemed successful, profitable enough for Sir John to purchase at his own expense the 40,000-ton RMS *Olympic* for £10,000. This was the second ship purchased by the scheme and sold to the breakers for a handsome profit. The only cash to come from the now dwindling Surrey Fund was the shared expense of dredging the dockside. For the miserly sum of £1,000, eighteen months work had been secured and provided for 200 men on the *Olympic* alone. Many more vessels including the RMS *Berengaria* and *Monarch of Bermuda* were broken up at Jarrow.

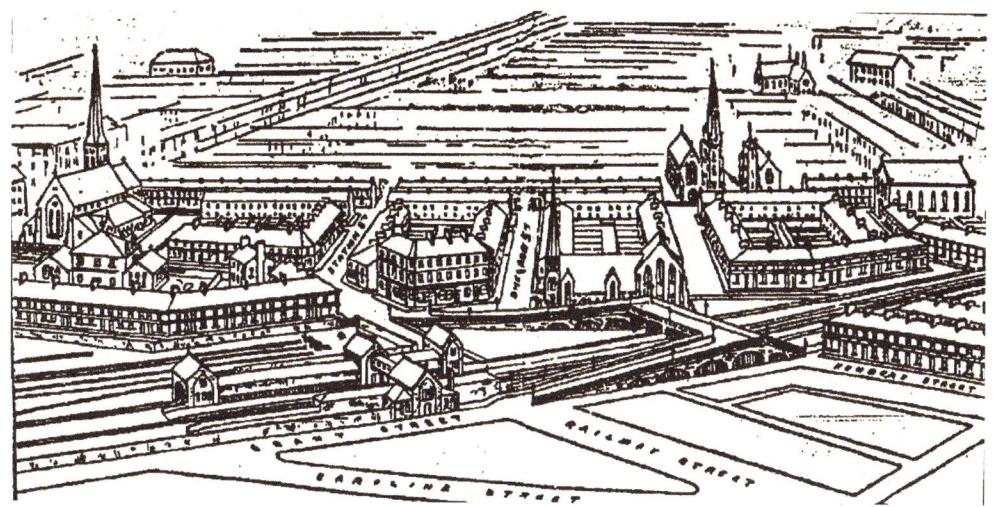

Proposed plan for the railway crossing.

Station Stairs

Similar to many other towns in the country that have grown rapidly, Jarrow had many needs. One in particular was the need for a bridge spanning the passenger and mineral lines at the railway station, linking both sides of the town. In 1884, a decision was taken to erect a stairway connecting the two points, which became known – not surprisingly – as the 'station stairs'. By 1891 plans were being prepared to elaborate upon the simple stairway, because of the danger it created during inclement weather. A glance at the accompanying illustration shows – almost without words – how this could be achieved. It was thought a bridge at this location would greatly reduce the distance between Albert Road and the town centre for horse-drawn vehicles and hand carts. The proposed 30-foot-wide crossing was to be constructed of concrete, reinforced with steel girders and have a total length of 520 feet including the approaches. A gradient of 1 in 13 at the Clayton Street approach and 1 in 12 at Grant Street was thought somewhat steep, but not steep enough to create problems and cause an impediment to traffic. Alas, an acute shortage of money prevented any further progress of the structure. Alternatively, the existing walkway was reinforced enough to support the weight of a glass-sided canopy, and remained this way until its demolition in the 1970s.

Sir John Jarvis

Prior to the welcome arrival of Sir John Jarvis and the Surrey Fund, a social centre for the unemployed had been organised in the disued paper mills at Springwell in 1934 by the churches at Westminster. The aim of the Surrey Fund was to bring fresh hope

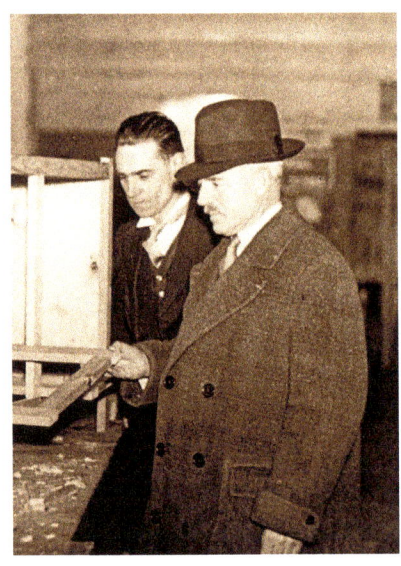

Sir John Jarvis, High Sheriff of Surrey, at the Jarrow Instruction Centre, 1935.

to the people of Tyneside, to provide them with pleasant surroundings and hopefully a brighter future, to teach them new skills, and ultimately find them permanent work. Sir John's first objective was Jarrow. The raw nature and fragility of the town revealed it to be the worst hit town in the country, with eight out of ten men out of work. These figures meant that the town had to move forward, with the help and careful direction from Jarvis and the £40,000 Surrey Fund he brought with him. The object of the fund was to ease the hardship of the people of Jarrow, especially the victims of the abrupt closure of Palmers. Sir John secured 50,000 items of clothing, bedding and the much needed children's clothing from a Personal Service League in the south. Jarrow was a crowded town during the 1930s, and the need for open spaces was deemed a vital necessity. Directed by Jarvis and the fund, 20 acres of parkland were created at Monkton Dene providing work for 1,000 unemployed men, each being employed for one calendar month, with preference going to those with dependent families. Most turned up for work with their feet so poorly shod that it prevented them from doing a satisfactory day's work, so each man was supplied with a new pair of quality boots – a total of 910 pairs of boots were supplied courtesy of the fund. In addition to the creation of the park, the men assisted in the erection of two cricket pavilions elsewhere in the town. From the very beginning, the success or failure of the Surrey Scheme depended upon the provision of permanent work; all of the ongoing activities were engineered towards this ultimate goal.

Simon Temple

Entrepreneur and industrialist Simon Temple was born in 1759 at Westoe, South Shields, into a wealthy family. His parents owned a small but prosperous shipbuilding business. By 1795 he acquired a substantial estate at Jarrow, which included St Paul's Church

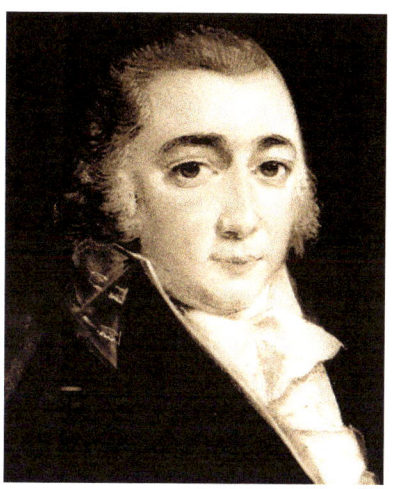

Entrepreneur and shipyard owner Simon Temple.

and its surrounding area. In 1798, he opened a new dry dock at the family shipbuilding yard, which at that particular time was the biggest and most efficient in the country. With a faithful workforce and full order book, the lucrative yard went from strength to strength, so much so the company had to turn away valuable orders. By this time Temple was incredibly wealthy and in 1785 he built Jarrow Hall as his private residence. Around this time, he turned his attention to other business interests and to the prospects of mining coal. In September 1803, after a grand inauguration ceremony, he opened the Alfred Pit at Jarrow, creating many hundreds of much-needed jobs. The first coal to be surfaced from the pit was shipped on board the *Fox* and transported to London – this was to herald the industrial growth of the town. He was a caring employer and did so much for the well-being of the people and lavished money on charitable causes. In 1804, he built row upon row of white-walled cottages in High Street and close to St Paul's Church for his faithful workforce. These cottages remained habitable until the 1930s when they were demolished. In 1811, with his vast wealth he purchased Hylton Castle, where he lived in style. In 1814, owing to mismanagement and by this time living above his means, his empire began to collapse around him due to unforeseen danger with the loss of many lives at the Alfred Pit, failing mining and shipyard investments, which led to his inevitable bankruptcy. Simon Temple died in 1822, aged sixty-three, at the home of one of his former manservants; a pitiful end to a great industrialist who contributed so much to the development of Jarrow. Currently, the old hall is used as a museum, Jarrow Hall, demonstrating life in Anglo-Saxon Britain.

Sir Charles Mark Palmer

Born in South Shields in 1822, Charles Palmer was the fourth son of a wealthy import and export merchant George Palmer. After a privileged upbringing, he commenced his education at the Bruce Academy in Newcastle, but completed it in Marseilles, France.

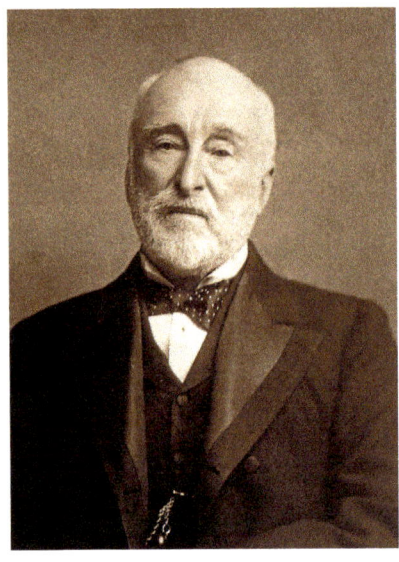

Sir Charles Mark Palmer Bart.

On his return to England in 1843, aged twenty-one, he joined his father's company, Palmer Beckwith & Co., who were active in the import and export of quality timber. However, the young and enterprising Charles had previously decided to earn his living in coal mining as demand for the inexpensive fuel was growing rapidly. In 1845, he was introduced to one of Britain's foremost coal owners John Bowes, who was so impressed by the young Palmer that he offered him employment. Within two years Palmer was made a managing partner of the firm. In 1852, together with his brother George, Charles created the General Iron Screw Collier Co. with capital of £250,000. The development of the shipbuilding company was rapid, and by 1857 a further £40,000 was invested in ironstone mines in North Yorkshire. In 1863, elder brother George retired from the company. Charles married his first wife Jane in 1846, and after her passing he married Augusta Mary Lambert in 1867. His third marriage to Gertrude Montgomery was in 1877. At the time of the creation of the borough of Jarrow in 1875 by HRH Queen Victoria, Palmer presented the town with a solid gold mayoral chain of office as a gesture to the recently formed town council, who deemed it appropriate that as Palmer was the founder of modern Jarrow he should be entrusted with the position of its first mayor. He accepted the position after careful consideration, and because of his many business interests, he could not give the position his full commitment, which resulted in Alderman Thomas Sheldon taking over the role. Palmer was overwhelmingly elected Member of Parliament for the town in 1885, and created a baron of the United Kingdom the following year. The caring businessman provided the Palmer Memorial Hospital in Clayton Street at his own expense in memory of his first wife Jane, and the Mechanics Institute in Ellison Street. In 1904, a statue dedicated to him was unveiled in the grounds of the hospital. He was decorated soon after the occasion with a knighthood for his commitment and services to industry. Sir Charles Mark Palmer passed away in 1907, and was interred in North Yorkshire.

Tyne Tunnels

Minister of Transport Right Honourable Alfred Barnes inaugurated the Tyne Pedestrian Tunnel Works. Work commenced simultaneously at both Jarrow and Howden on the north bank with the aim of meeting in the middle. The work went according to plan with the breakthrough on target and ahead of schedule 90 feet

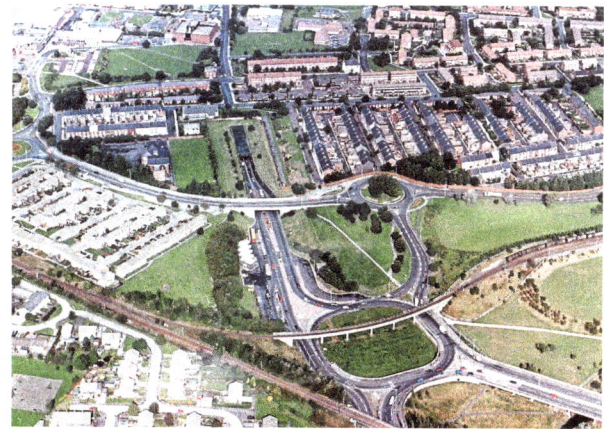

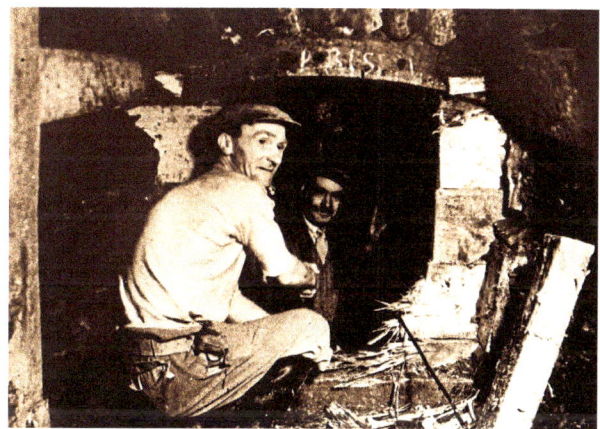

Jarrow entrance, exit and approach roads to the Tyne Tunnel, and construction of pedestrian tunnel from 1951.

below the river. Three tunnels were constructed, each 300 yards in length, one each for pedestrians and cyclists and the third used as a service tunnel. Entry and exit from the twin tunnels was by escalator for foot passengers, and elevator for wheelchairs and perambulators. By the late 1950s the tired old ferry service between Jarrow and Howden was unable to cope with the ever-increasing volumes of traffic. Work commenced on the Tyne road crossing between Jarrow and Howden again after years of wrangling as to where the new Tyne crossing should be located. The project finally got underway in 1960 at a cost of £8.5 million, with a further £3.5 million set aside for the approach roads. A toll was introduced to offset the cost of the many millions spent on the 5,500-foot-long tunnel by Northumberland and Durham County Councils, together with a government contribution. Her Majesty Elizabeth II performed the opening ceremony on 19 October 1967. In 2012, Her Majesty returned to the area to perform the opening ceremony for a sister tunnel.

Timber and Chemical Industries

Jarrow has been associated with the timber trade since the 1870s. Several companies were attracted to the area between east Jarrow and Tyne Dock for the purpose of supplying the coal mining industry with pit props. Pyman Bell traded here from 1873 exporting coal until the beginning of the twentieth century. From then and until the mines were nationalised in 1947, the company supplied the industry with

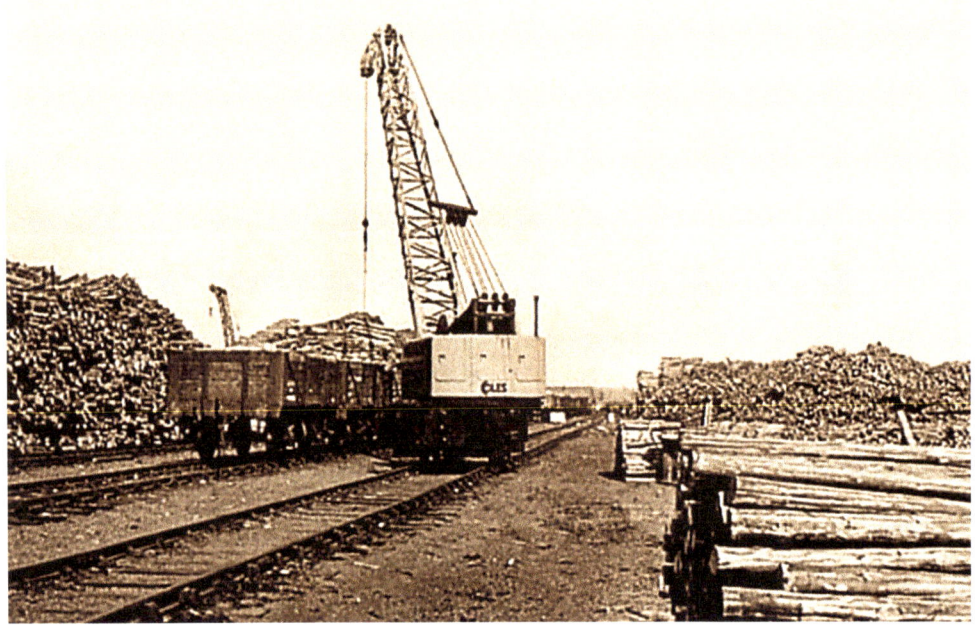

Denny Mott & Dickson timber yards, 1960.

mining timber from various locations in the north-east. The 1950s saw the timber industry supply fewer coal fields as mining became more mechanised, and from this time the company traded solely in sawn wood. Another company attracted to Jarrow was Matthew Southern & Co., who came to their present site from Newcastle in 1963. Originally the 3.5-acre site was adequate for their needs, but with the growing demand for timber and the increasing number of sawmills, storage sheds and timber treatment plants needed, the company today utilises 5.5 acres of the riverside. Prior to the invasion of the army of timber merchants, east Jarrow was predominantly occupied by the chemical industry from around 1845. The first of the chemical plants was Jefferson's situated close to Quay Corner, which manufactured sulphur for matches, disinfectants and bleach, who were easily recognised by the pollution billowing from its two tall chimneys. The construction of two further plants followed after the success of Jefferson's, Kenmire's and Richardson's, but on a much bigger scale, supplying raw materials to many national and international companies. These industries flourished in Jarrow for many years employing almost all of the male working population of east Jarrow. A recession in the chemical industry during the 1930s and the intrusion of foreign competition eventually forced the companies out of business.

Tram Service

Travelling facilities in Jarrow prior to the beginning of the twentieth century were virtually non-existent up until the inauguration of the tram service, and it was no mean feat to journey to either Sunderland or Newcastle; beyond these boundaries was almost impossible. A market boat travelled to Newcastle on a Saturday morning. Several sandbanks and debris in the river made this a perilous trip. A ferry joining Howden with Jarrow operated in the form of a sculler boat, the fare for the unreliable and dangerous trip was anything between two pence to half a crown, dependent on the time of day, wind direction, the tide or the sobriety of the oarsman. By 1900, the population of the town and prosperity had grown beyond all expectations due to the industrial boom Jarrow was experiencing. The need for a reliable transport system was deemed necessary to shuttle the men to and from work, the electric tramcar was looked upon favourably as the efficiency of systems in other towns was carefully monitored. The Jarrow tram service, if it was to go ahead, was to be both convenient and economically viable to operate smoothly and efficiently. After several months of debating possible complications, work began on the £60,000 transport system in 1901. A vast network of tramlines snaked their way from the sheds at Tyne Dock where the cars were garaged, to Western Road where the service terminated. Upon completion, the efficient system was powered by coal fired, steam driven generators from a power station in Beech Street. Passengers wishing to travel beyond this point could do so with the aid of horse drawn buses,

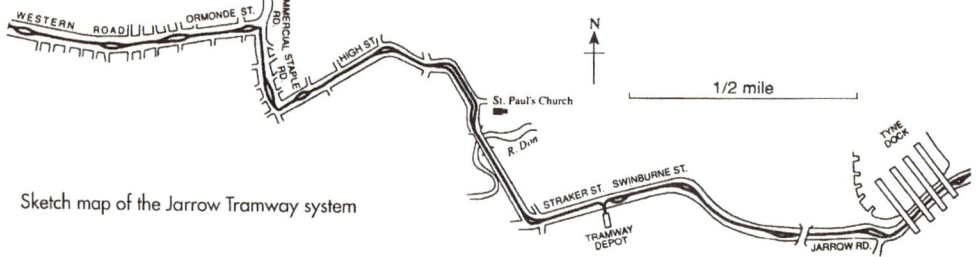

Sketch map of the Jarrow Tramway system

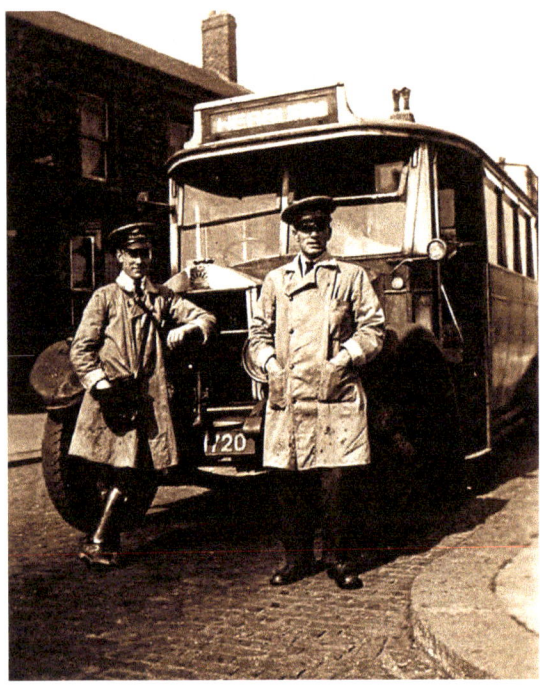

Above and left: Route of Jarrow tram service from 1906. The tram service was superseded by Charlton's buses from 1929.

which operated in conjunction with the service. The first trial car of the Jarrow & District Electric Traction Co. Ltd was car No 5. The tram service was discontinued in 1929 at the arrival of the motorbus.

Trains, Boats and Reins

The former railway station in Jarrow was situated in Grant Street. The rail link between Pelaw and South Shields opened in March 1872. Prior to this time the line operated a service from a junction close to the location of the current metro station at Pelaw. The goods-only service operated on a mineral line through Monkton village to a station close to Wylam Street, which could account for the obscure position of the street and the rectangular street plan around it. Because of its proximity to the river and easy access to the vessels upon it, esparto grass from Spain was shipped in and transported

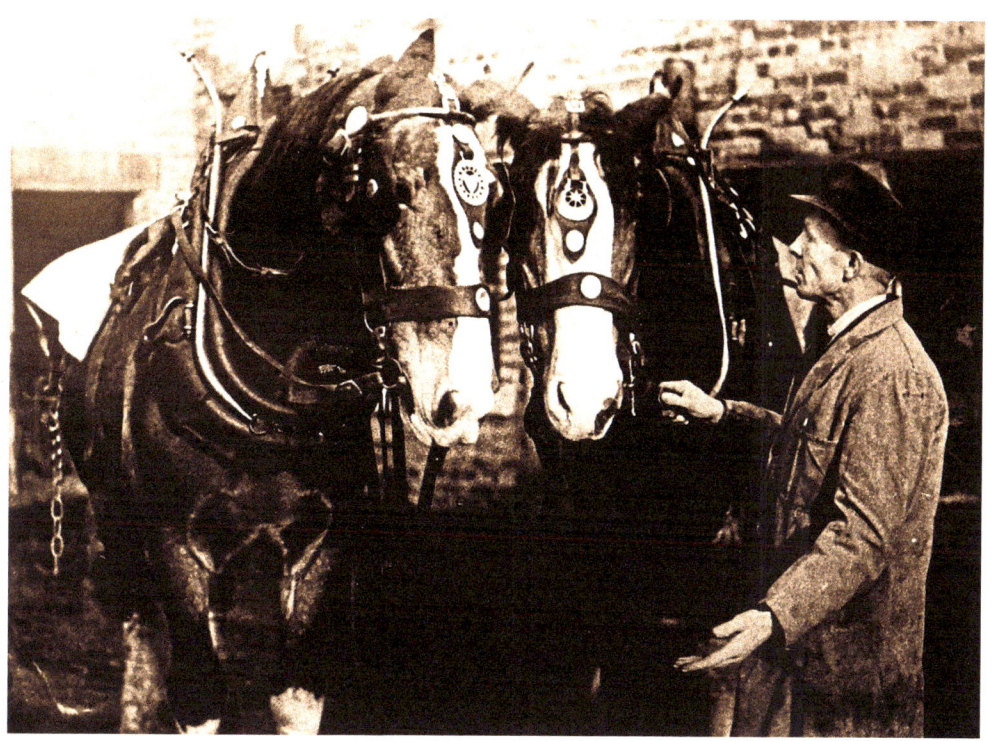

Shire horses Peggy and Sandy, retiring after twelve years with Jarrow & Hebburn Co-operative Society.

via another rail link to the paper mill at Springwell. A light railway system carrying fuel oil and goods was in operation from its inauguration in 1929, from the Grant Street station terminating at the east end of the town. Above all, and among its many attributes, what Jarovians did extremely well was to build ships. Prior to his death in 1907, Sir Charles Mark Palmer moulded his men, teaching them everything there was to know about the shipbuilding industry. They had a comprehensive knowledge of every craft on the waterways of the world, with a personal guarantee no finer vessels were available anywhere. Their expertise was reflected in the many hundreds of ships that sailed from the Tyne over in excess of eighty years. Brake and charabanc trips were fashionable around the beginning of the twentieth century; the horse-drawn vehicles were a common site up until the 1940s, along with an assortment of similar horse-drawn carts and trailers. Jarrow & Hebburn Co-operative Society made daily deliveries of bread, milk and fruit and vegetables this way up until the 1950s, from stables located at Hope Street. Peggy and Sandy, two shire horses, retired to assist in agricultural duties after twelve years of service with Jarrow Corporation cleansing department, pulling the heavy dust carts through the streets of Jarrow until the 1940s. Although extremely reliable, this type of transportation was costly and cumbersome.

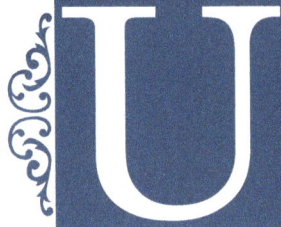

Unemployment

Jarvis Park lies juxtaposed with Springwell Park and serves as a memorial to Sir John Jarvis, who came to Jarrow during those bleak and desperate days of the 1930s, bringing with him the Surrey Fund. This fund was generously donated by the people of Surrey to help feed and clothe the people of Jarrow during those terrible years of the depression. Jarvis, who embraced the town, was the driving force behind the creation of the Jarrow Instruction Centre, based at the disused paper mill at Springwell. The objective of the centre was to teach the unemployed of the town new skills. Unemployment was at its highest in Jarrow during the 1930s with 80 per cent of the male working population out of work. The recent closure of our precious shipyard was to have a devastating effect on most other businesses in the town. The situation was to become progressively worse, so bad in fact that in 1936 town MP Ellen Wilkinson chose 200 men hungry for work to march 250 miles to London with a petition of 10,000 signatures in an attempt to inform Prime Minister Stanley Baldwin and his government of the plight of our town. Somewhat disillusioned, the men returned to Jarrow to the street corners to which they had become so familiar with very few prospects. The government's abrupt and unsympathetic refusal of assistance was a further blow to these proud men who were simply fighting for the right to feed their families.

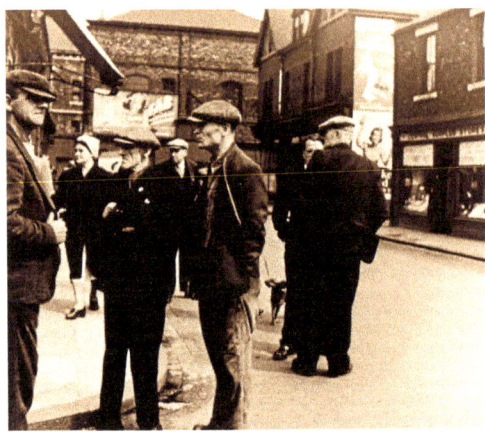

Unemployed workers, Market Square, 1935.

V

Venerable Bede

Growing up at the Abbey of St Peter at Monkwearmouth was a child called Bede who was devoted to the service of the Lord and called by Him to do greater things. Bede had previously commenced his education at St Peter's, and by the age of twelve was installed with the brethren at the monastery at Jarrow. This child whose whole life was spent among the cloisters and church at Jarrow grew to be a man of wide learning, humility, piety, scholarship and science. In his cell was the lamp of English Learning, which attracted scholars from all parts of England and far-off Europe. Bede's works are voluminous and varied, mastering all that was known in his time. The forty-five works he left us, apart from various theological pieces, included music, philosophy, grammar, rhetoric, arithmetic and medicine, an incredible encyclopaedia of knowledge. He was a skilled musician, and possessed the rare accomplishments of speaking fluently and writing Greek, Hebrew and Latin. His *Ecclesiastical History of the English Nation* rapidly spread his reputation throughout Christian Europe.

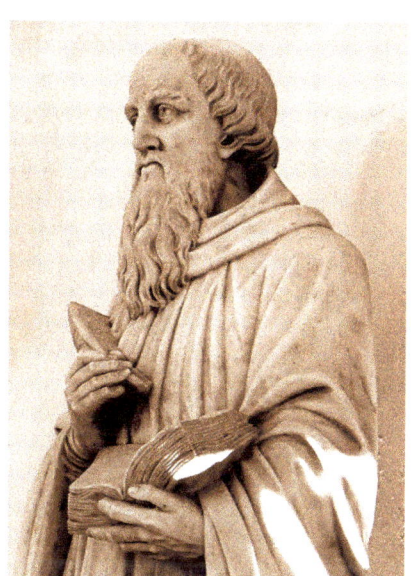

Right and overleaf: Statue to the Venerable Bede, and an engraving of his passing on 26 May AD 735.

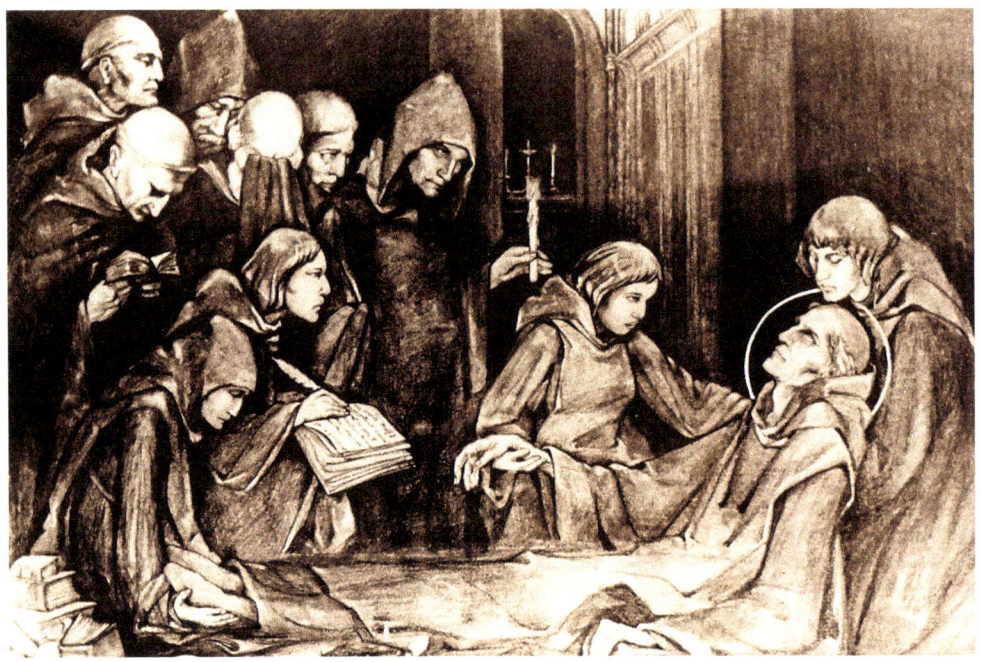

From this insignificant little abbey on the edge of Christian civilisation, Bede dominated the intellectual brains of Europe. His final work the translation of St John's Gospel into English was carried out with painful suffering and ailing health. The great man who toiled for the benefit of the English nation and his fellow brethren died of asthma aged sixty-two on 26 May AD 735. He became the town's most celebrated resident, and one of the most remarkable men this country has ever produced. His remains are entombed in a sepulchre at Durham Cathedral.

Valentine Linsley

Another of the town's memorable and much-loved sons was Valentine Linsley. Born in Jarrow into an Anglo-Italian family in 1938, the eldest of six children, Val was the oldest son of Theresa and John Linsley, grandson to Marta and Salvatore Rea, and was named in memory of his uncle Valentino Rea. From the family home in Albert Road, Val commenced his education in 1943 at St Bede's Secondary Modern School in the town, and similar to most St Bede's boys of the era, he showed a promising aptitude in football. On completion of his education in 1955, he decided he wanted to earn his living as an electrical and mechanical engineer at Vickers Armstrong in Gateshead. In order to satisfy his love and passion for ships, Val completed his apprenticeship at sea in 1959. Back on dry land, he worked in many of the shipyards that lined either side of the River Tyne. He particularly enjoyed the many sea trials he was involved with. His final trip was aboard HMS *Ark Royal* in 2001. Aged eighteen, Val fell head over heels

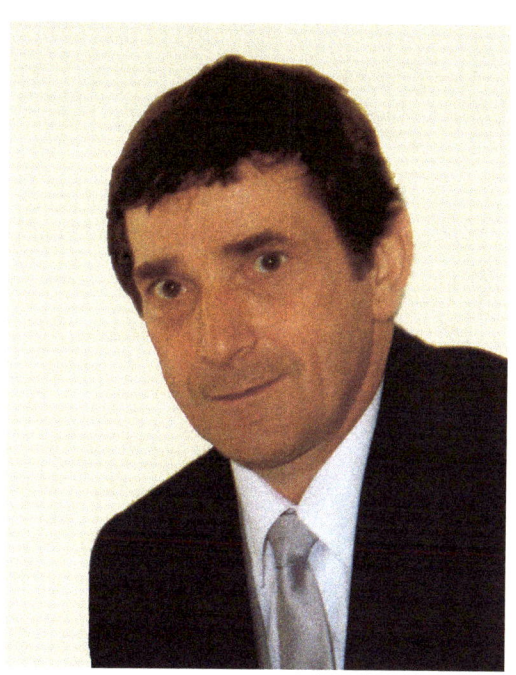

Valentine Linsley, one of the town's well-known and respected characters.

for Christine Potter when they first met at the local hop at the Mechanics Institute in Ellison Street. They married in London in 1965 and soon after they returned to their roots in Jarrow. Christine gave birth to two daughters, Christina and Maria, who gave the couple four beautiful grandchildren: Thereze, Kieran, Gabriella and Dominic. Multi-talented, charismatic and proud of his Italian heritage, Val became master of ceremonies at St Bede's Club in the town, and often entertained, crooning songs made famous by another two memorable Italians, Dean Martin and Frank Sinatra. Football-crazy Val assisted in the organisation and running of local Sunday morning league games, was an ardent supporter of Newcastle United, and, of course, followed the progress of his two grandsons Kieran and Dominic, offering advice whenever required. He enjoyed friendly banter about the game with his two sons in law Kevin and Anth. A devoted Catholic, Val preyed regularly at his parish church. Most of the time it was for 'Rain in California' as the jovial character's idea of heaven was being surrounded by his devoted family, a large glass of red wine and an enormous plate of Spaghetti Bolognese – that's amore.

Viking Invasions

The Viking age is a period in history dating from the eighth to the eleventh centuries. It was around this time that the Scandinavian warriors explored Europe by the seas and rivers surrounding it for the purpose of trade and conquest. These Vikings were recognised as brutal raiders and murderers by the populations they visited throughout

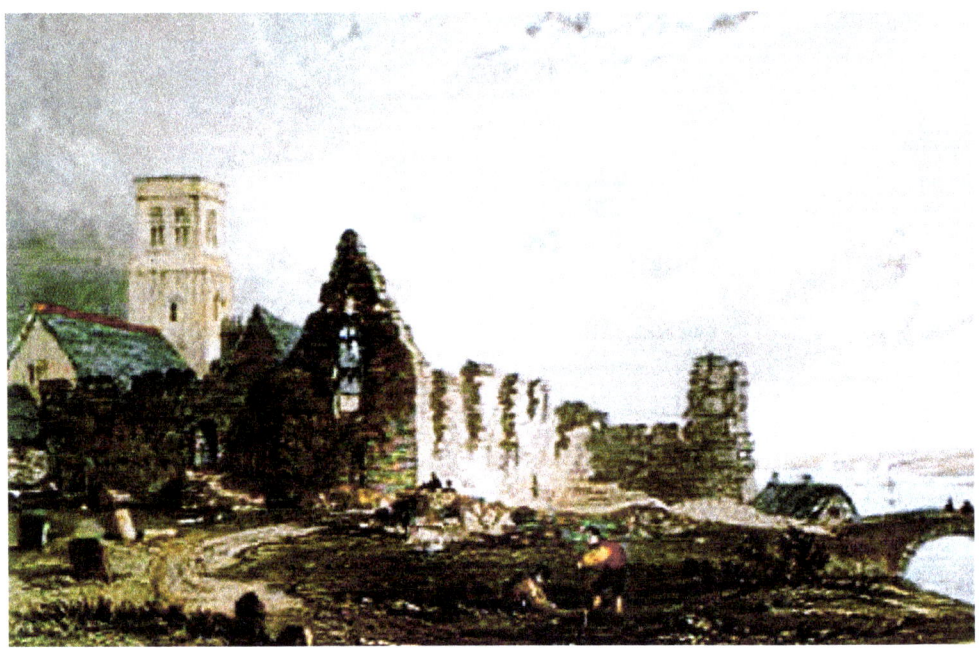

Monastery ruins at the time of the Viking invasions.

Eastern and Western Europe. Around AD 794, the invading warriors beached their longboats at Lindisfarne Island just off the Northumberland coast, devastating the abbey that at that time was an important centre of learning for monks and scholars. Many of the holy Island's monks and priests were either slain or carried off for slavery. This wanton looting, pillaging and devastation continued on many coastal areas of this country. It was during the second invasion by the Danes to Northumbria in AD 866 that both monasteries at Wearmouth and Jarrow were devastated by fire. Jarrow was so severely hit that it had to be abandoned, and lay derelict and desolate for close to 150 years. In the subsequent years many attempts were made to restore the Jarrow monastery; a determined attempt was made by Walcher Bishop of Durham in 1075, but this was unsuccessful. As the centuries passed, further attempts were made to restore the decaying monastery, but the savage northern weather had taken its toll on the building, which had suffered irreparable damage. Its Roman and Saxon ruins have since lain undisturbed.

W

Waterfront

For centuries the River Tyne has been the lifeblood and backbone of many communities who earned their living from its waters. The mighty Tyne has two major tributaries: the first in the north rises from the most northerly reaches of the Cheviot Hills, while the southern region of the waterway rises in the Pennines, prior to it flowing to the heart of industrial Tyneside, and eventually into the raging waters of the North Sea. The waterfront at Jarrow has been in existence since Anglo-Saxon times, and together with the River Don surrounded Jarrow when it was not much more than a tiny village. This we can ascertain from ancient maps and records, which reveal that the Romans anchored their vessels at the mouth of the River Don twice, King Egfrid sheltered the whole of his fleet here, and afterwards the marauding Danes moored their longboats in the Tyne Estuary on more than one occasion during the eighth and ninth centuries. Though the history from these times is somewhat fragmentary, what we do know is the

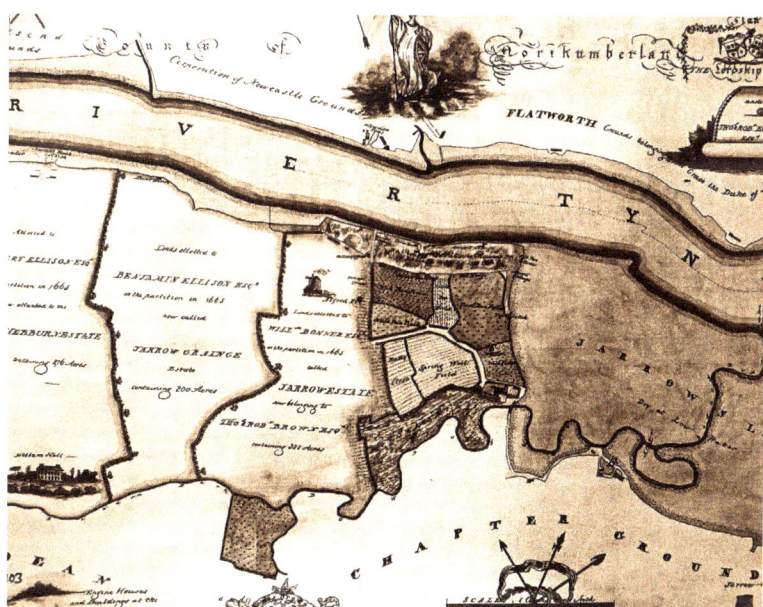

The waterfront at Jarrow around 1760.

Don was not the little waterway it is today, being big enough to accommodate several vessels. This was, of course, long before both rivers became polluted with many years of industrialisation. In recent times, fishing with rod and line from the embankments was more for entertainment, rather than to put a meal on the table, due to the polluted waters. During the eighth century, fishing for the table was very much a way of life in these salmon-rich and crystal clear waters. In excess of 2,000 salmon were taken from the Tyne in one day, and sold at a Newcastle market for the equivalent of 2p per lb in 1760.

Wartime Jarrow

Forty minutes after the city of Newcastle was severely damaged as a result of an air attack during the Second World War, and after missing its Tyne Bridge target, the enemy turned its attention to industry along the length of the river east of the city. The Mercantile Dry Dock and fuel storage tanks at the Shell depot in east Jarrow were the designated targets of the Luftwaffe in this heavily industrialised part of Tyneside. Luckily the targets were missed completely, suffering only minimal fire damage, which was rapidly brought under control. Jarrow would surely have been devastated should the primary targets have been hit. Sadly, and unfortunately, the nearby Princess Street took the direct hit, which wiped out ten residences on 2 July 1940, claiming upwards of twenty lives and injuring as many as 120. ARP workers, firemen and volunteers toiled relentlessly through the night searching the debris for casualties. These were the first of many fatalities of the war years in Jarrow – Dunn Street School was damaged beyond repair in the same attack. Another successful mission for the Luftwaffe was a night raid on Sheldon Street and the adjoining Station Street in 1941, when dozens of houses were destroyed with twenty-four fatalities and twenty-eight injuries, nine of which were serious. In the same raid an infant school in Grant Street was so severely damaged and subsequently demolished.

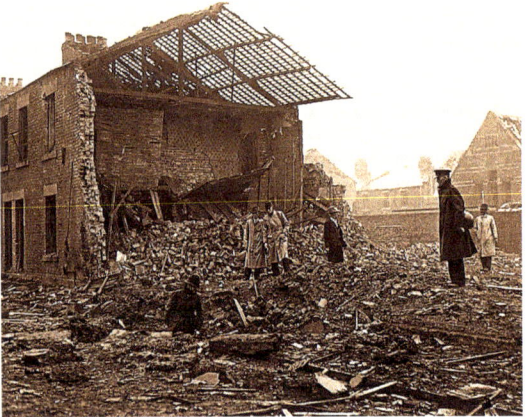 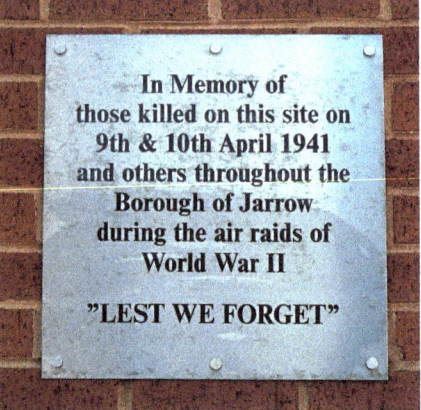

Bomb damage in the town centre in 1940, and commemorative plaque.

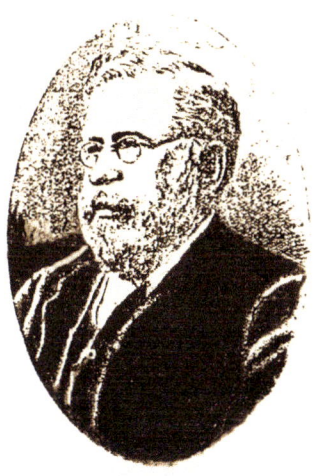

Paper mill owner and educationalist William Henry
Richardson JP.

WILLIAM HENRY RICHARDSON, J.P.,
Chairman of the first School Board.

William Henry Richardson

Education facilities grew in the early part of the nineteenth century along with the
expanding industry and population. The town's first school, Bede Parochial of 1840, was
located on land between St Paul's Church and monastery ruins. It was paper mill owner
William Henry Richardson's enthusiasm that was instrumental in bringing formal
education to Jarrow. He was the driving force behind the creation of the country's first
board school. Dedicated to the cause, in March 1871 he was deservedly rewarded with the
responsible position as chairman of the recently formed Hedworth Monkton & Jarrow
School Board. The school was housed in a disused theatre in Drury Lane with John Witter
appointed as head. Prior to the creation of the Education Act, it seemed any building with
four walls and a roof was adequate and satisfactory for the education of young children.
Following a series of devastating fires at the paper mill, a severe slump in the industry and
the untimely and accidental death of Richardson in 1923 at his home Monkton Lodge, the
ailing mill was sold and eventually dismantled inevitably, adding to Jarrow's growing list of
failing industries. Through the subsequent years the disused mill became the temporary
home to the Jarrow Instruction Centre, which was set up to teach the unemployed new
skills. By 1960 Smith's furnishing group used the outbuildings as warehouses and offices.
After the evacuation of its final resident Kenton Utilities in March 1998, the remainder of
the property was demolished in favour of the Mill Dene housing complex.

Wesleyan Movement

During 1860, the Wesleyan movement and various other religions were developing
in the town. The huge influxes of migrants from other regions were attracted to the

shipyards and what the town had to offer. Many of these immigrants came from religious backgrounds, which the heads of the various denominations instantly recognised and promptly acted upon. The Wesleyans constructed a chapel in the Market Square in 1861. The foundation stone was laid by Charles Mark Palmer, who also donated £50 towards building costs, and another £50 towards the cost of a Sunday school. The massive increase in the population of the town made it necessary to build a day school. In 1867, a site was purchased next to the chapel for £92 for the construction of the school, as there were no grants of any description available at this time from the government, Education Departments or the Wesleyan Chapel Building Committee. The revenue was raised by public subscription among local Methodists. By 1870 the growth of the town caused it to spread in all directions and the trustees of the chapel felt it was no longer central to the community. After the sale of the chapel the revenue was used to construct a more substantial church closer to the centre of town. The foundation stone was laid by Palmer in 1870 on the site of a former school dating from 1860. The school offered private education to those who could afford the fees, and formed the basis of the Kings School at Tynemouth. The 800-seat church on a triangular site at the junction of Albert Road and St John's Terrace was ready for worshippers by 1872. The opening ceremony of the £3,000 church was attended by a large crowd of well-wishers from the Wesleyan movement.

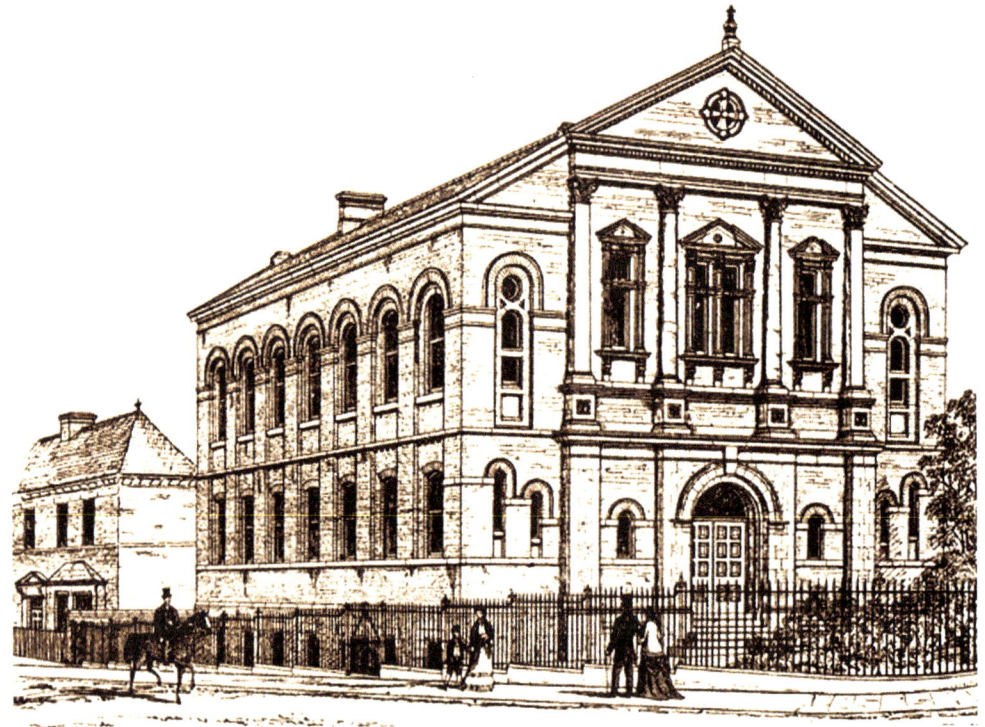

St John's Church.

X

Xylography

Initially when I came to associate 'X' with Jarrow, I dismissed it in order to tackle it alone after working my way through the remainder of the alphabet. Every so often the daunting thought of 'X' came to mind. 'X', just like every other letter in the alphabet, could stand alone but quite often for it to make any sense it was prefixed with another letter, generally a vowel that in nine cases out of ten was 'E'. However, for millennia 'X' has been the Roman symbol for ten, and is recognised on ancient treasure maps to mark a particular spot where a hoard was buried. 'X' was legally accepted centuries ago as a signature when learning to read and write was difficult for some, and is often used to signify an unspecified number, 'X' has always been recognised as a symbol of a term of endearment in the form of a kiss, and it was used decades ago to 'spot the ball' in competitions. It has also been, it seems, since the beginning of time used in the tried and tested method when casting a vote on a ballot paper; apparently fewer errors are made when counting crosses. Together with the prefix 'E' it has become known as a former lover. An American punk rock band called simply 'X' surfaced during the 1970s. It was also used to signify when a film was for adult viewing only; the 'X' men graced the big screen in 2000; in 2001 the Xbox became the latest craze for the young and not so young; and in 2004 the 'X' factor talent show zoomed into our living rooms via television. Today, 'X' is often used as a full stop when texting. It is also worth mentioning that there was a private members' club in Market Square around 1910 called the Excelsior. However, I bring your attention to the work of Peter Winstanley, a xylographer employed by the town's newspapers the *Jarrow Express* and the *Guardian*. The work of the xylographer was to engrave the wooden blocks used to illustrate the news during the production of the broadsheet, prior to the photographic process being adapted for use in photo journalism.

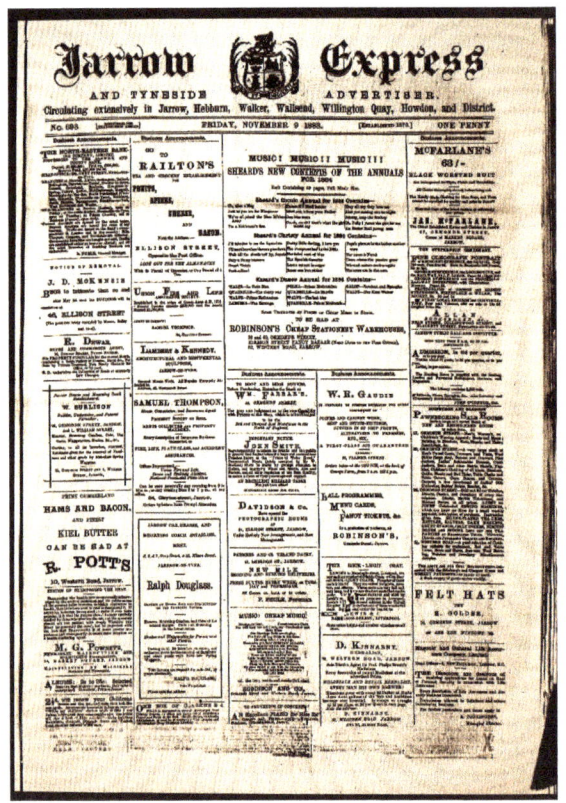

Above and below: *Jarrow Express* and the detailed work of the xylographer in this image of the town hall.

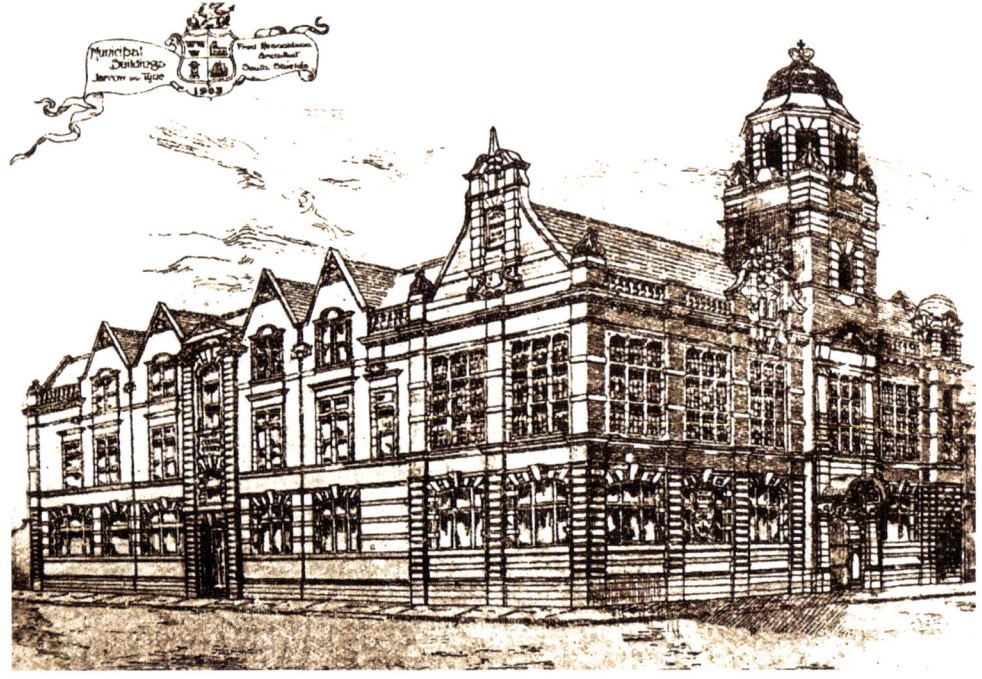

Y

Youth Clubs

Youth clubs are places with a controlled environment where young people meet and participate in a variety of activities, such as table tennis and video games, and these clubs often offer a fitness programme to those interested. Youth clubs were established around 1911, and designed to keep bored adolescents off the streets and out of trouble. In the United Kingdom, there are a number of national youth club networks, which include the National Association of Boys and Girls Clubs, many of which are open to all from the ages of ten to twenty-one, and all steering towards the same goal to help and offer advice to its members, and help them understand the world around them. The trained youth leaders and workers would guide them through varying activities and schemes similar to the Duke of Edinburgh Award programme. His Royal Highness George V had a genuine interest in such clubs, so much so he was behind such a club created in Jarrow High Street in 1934. Prior to this a similar club for fourteen to sixteen-year-old boys was underway at Chapel Road, which later moved to bigger premises, Acca House in Grant Street, after the Second World War, and for a time was active under the name of the Saxon Club, until the building was devastated by fire and subsequently demolished in 1973.

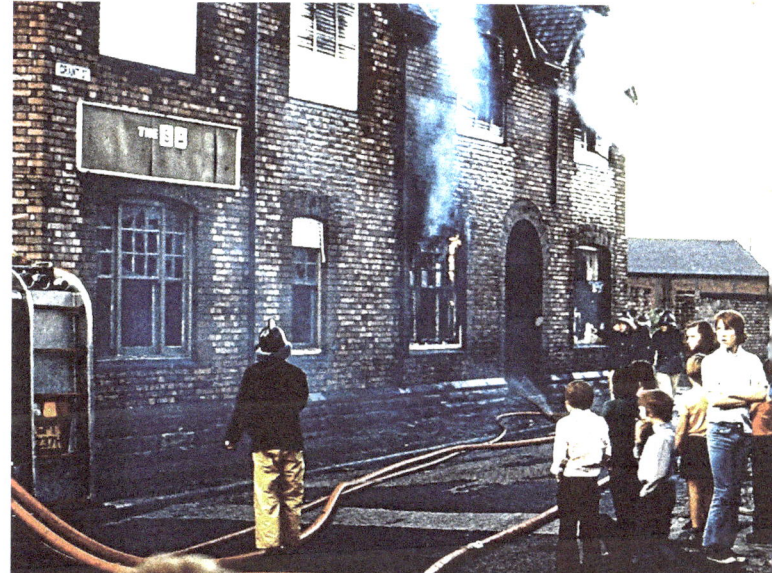

Remnants of Acca House and Saxon Youth Club, Grant Street.

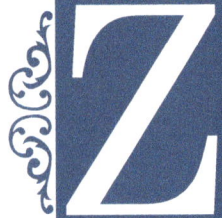

Zephaniah Harris

Zephaniah Harris was born in Norfolk in 1836, but settled in Jarrow towards the middle of the nineteenth century, setting himself up as a successful businessman in the building trade. In 1883, he invested the profits from his building business in wine and beer retailing in Western Road. After applying successfully for election as a governor on the Jarrow Burial Board, he stood for council election in 1886, and after being nominated for three wards, eventually he was elected to serve the Jarrow Ward and successfully elected as mayor of the town in 1891, while being an active member of the judicial system as a Justice of the Peace. He married Sarah Thompson on 26 December 1898, setting up home in a fine residence he built at Albert Road. He fathered two daughters Sarah and Mary and a son Stephen. In 1905, he ventured into the world of antiques and auctioneering from premises in Bede Burn Road, which he shared with his estate agent brother William Gladstone Harris. After retiring from his many business interests around 1906, he concentrated his efforts on council and formal duties. He eventually sold the house in Albert Road to his estate agent brother, who resided there until 1923, when it was purchased by a physician who resided there until 1935. From this time the property was converted into the Alberta Social Club and remained so until its demolition in 1980. Kingfisher Lodge was constructed on the vacant site soon after and designed in a similar style to that of the former residence.

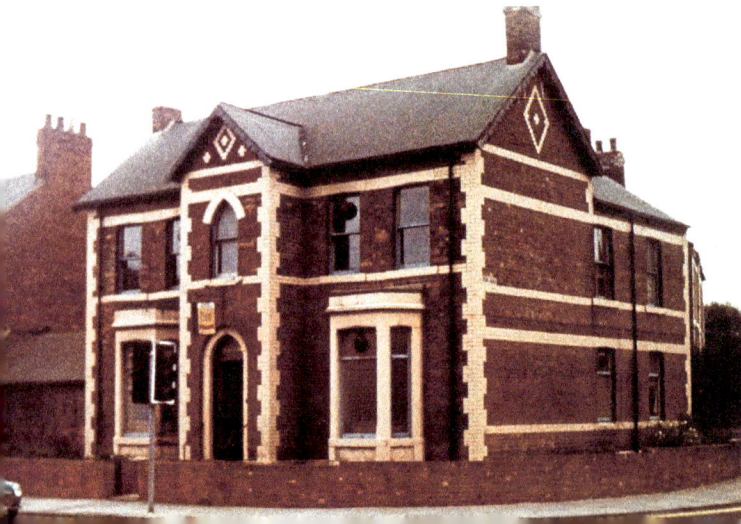

Zephaniah Harris's residence in Albert Road, which became the Alberta Social Club.